PRACTICAL WITCH'S ALMANAC
Walking Your Path
This edition © Microcosm Publishing, 2019
First published September, 2019
ISBN 978-1-62106-065-9
This is Microcosm #.496

2020 / 23rd Edition

The 2020 Practical Witch's Almanac: Walking Your Path
Copyright © 2019 Friday Gladheart, PracticalWitch.com

For a catalog, write or visit:
Microcosm Publishing
2752 N Williams Ave.
Portland, OR 97227
(503)799-2698
Microcosm.Pub

To join the ranks of high-class stores that feature Microcosm titles, talk to your rep: In the U.S. Como (Atlantic), Fujii (Midwest), Book Travelers West (Pacific), Turnaround in Europe, Manda/UTP in Canada, New South in Australia, and GPS in Asia, India, Africa, and South America.

If you bought this on Amazon, I'm so sorry because you could have gotten it cheaper and supported a small, independent publisher at Microcosm.Pub

Global labor conditions are bad, and our roots in industrial Cleveland in the 70s and 80s made us appreciate the need to treat workers right. Therefore, our books are MADE IN THE USA and printed on post-consumer paper.

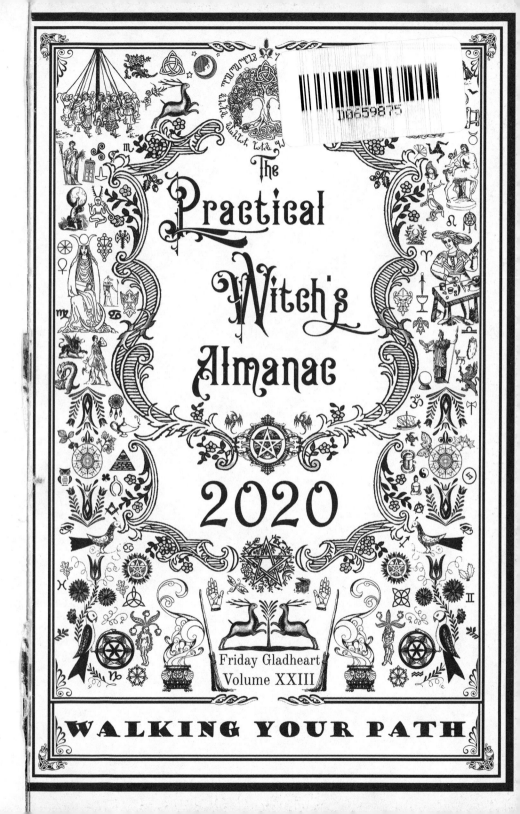

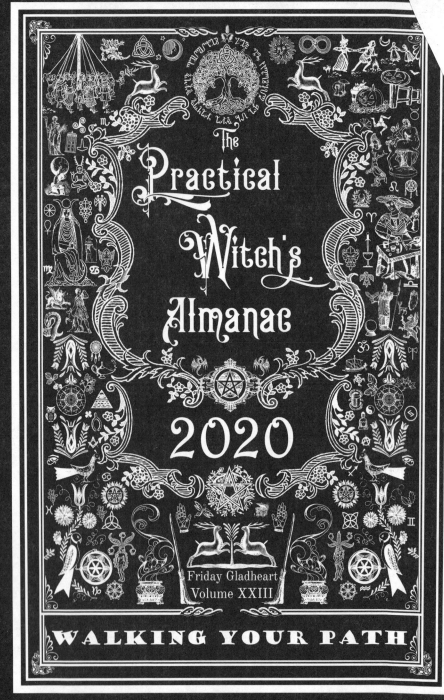

The
Practical
Witch's
Almanac

2020

Friday Gladheart
Volume XXIII

WALKING YOUR PATH

Friday Gladheart

Microcosm Publishing
Portland, Ore

MICROCOSM · PUBLISHING

Microcosm Publishing is Portland's most diversified publishing house and distributor with a focus on the colorful, authentic, and empowering. Our books and zines have put your power in your hands since 1996, equipping readers to make positive changes in their lives and in the world around them. Microcosm emphasizes skill-building, showing hidden histories, and fostering creativity through challenging conventional publishing wisdom with books and bookettes about DIY skills, food, bicycling, gender, self-care, and social justice. What was once a distro and record label was started by Joe Biel in his bedroom and has become among the oldest independent publishing houses in Portland, OR. We are a politically moderate, centrist publisher in a world that has inched to the right for the past 80 years.

2020 Weekly Index

January

Week	Mo	Tu	We	Th	Fr	Sa	Su
1			1	2	3	4	5
2	6	7	8	9	10	11	12
3	13	14	15	16	17	18	19
4	20	21	22	23	24	25	26
5	27	28	29	30	31		

2 ◐ 10 ○ 17 ◑ 24 ●

February

Week	Mo	Tu	We	Th	Fr	Sa	Su
5						1	2
6	3	4	5	6	7	8	9
7	10	11	12	13	14	15	16
8	17	18	19	20	21	22	23
9	24	25	26	27	28	29	

1 ◐ 9 ○ 15 ◑ 23 ●

March

Week	Mo	Tu	We	Th	Fr	Sa	Su
9							1
10	2	3	4	5	6	7	8
11	9	10	11	12	13	14	15
12	16	17	18	**19**	20	21	22
13	23	24	25	26	27	28	29
14	30	31					

2 ◐ 9 ○ 16 ◑ 24 ●

April

Week	Mo	Tu	We	Th	Fr	Sa	Su
14			1	2	3	4	5
15	6	7	8	9	10	11	12
16	13	14	15	16	17	18	19
17	20	21	22	23	24	25	26
18	27	28	29	**30**			

1 ◐ 7 ○ 14 ◑ 22 ● 30 ◐

May

Week	Mo	Tu	We	Th	Fr	Sa	Su
18					**1**	2	3
19	**4**	5	6	7	8	9	10
20	11	12	13	14	15	16	17
21	18	19	20	21	22	23	24
22	25	26	27	28	29	30	31

7:○ 14:◑ 22:● 29:◐

June

Week	Mo	Tu	We	Th	Fr	Sa	Su
23	1	2	3	4	5	6	7
24	8	9	10	11	12	13	14
25	15	16	17	18	19	**20**	21
26	22	23	24	25	26	27	28
27	29	30					

5 ○ 13 ◑ 21 ● 28 ◐

Dates in **bold** correspond to Sabbats, see the Wheel of the Year (inside covers).

Constellations & Zodiac Signs

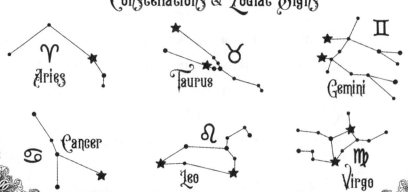

2020 Weekly Index

July

Week	Mo	Tu	We	Th	Fr	Sa	Su
27			1	2	3	4	5
28	6	7	8	9	10	11	12
29	13	14	15	16	17	18	19
30	20	21	22	23	24	25	26
31	27	28	29	30	31		

5 ○   12 ◑   20 ●   27 ◐

August

Week	Mo	Tu	We	Th	Fr	Sa	Su
31						**1**	2
32	3	4	5	**6**	7	8	9
33	10	11	12	13	14	15	16
34	17	18	19	20	21	22	23
35	24	25	26	27	28	29	30
36	31						

3 ○   11 ◑   18 ●   25 ◐

September

Week	Mo	Tu	We	Th	Fr	Sa	Su
36		1	2	3	4	5	6
37	7	8	9	10	11	12	13
38	14	15	16	17	18	19	20
39	21	**22**	23	24	25	26	27
40	28	29	30				

2 ○   10 ◑   17 ●   23 ◐

October

Week	Mo	Tu	We	Th	Fr	Sa	Su
40				1	2	3	4
41	5	6	7	8	9	10	11
42	12	13	14	15	16	17	18
43	19	20	21	22	23	24	25
44	26	27	28	29	30	**31**	

1 ○   9 ◑   16 ●   23 ◐   31 ○

November

Week	Mo	Tu	We	Th	Fr	Sa	Su
44							1
45	2	3	4	5	6	**7**	8
46	9	10	11	12	13	14	15
47	16	17	18	19	20	21	22
48	23	24	25	26	27	28	29
49	30						

8 ◑   15 ●   21 ◐   30 ○

December

Week	Mo	Tu	We	Th	Fr	Sa	Su
49		1	2	3	4	5	6
50	7	8	9	10	11	12	13
51	14	15	16	17	18	19	**20**
52	21	22	23	24	25	26	27
53	28	29	30	31			

7 ◐   14 ●   21 ◑   29 ○

Dates in **bold** correspond to Sabbats, see the Wheel of the Year (inside covers).

Constellations & Zodiac Signs

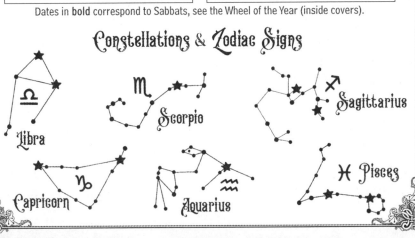

♎ Libra
♏ Scorpio
♐ Sagittarius
♑ Capricorn
♒ Aquarius
♓ Pisces

Table of Contents

*Let there be beauty and strength
power and compassion, honor
and humility, mirth and
reverence within you.*[1]

Welcome

Welcome to the 23rd edition! Thank you for choosing this almanac as your personal companion for the year. This edition is all about choosing and practicing your own unique path and is designed to help you reach your goals, learn, and develop in your own way.

The diversity of individuals who identify as Witches is astounding. From January 2018 to March 2019, hundreds of interviews and surveys were compiled in order to share with you this varied tapestry that keeps Witches a strong and persistent presence in the world. You will discover the empowering stories others have shared to inspire you to confidently walk your own path.

Witches are uniquely understanding of persecution and we embrace our diversity. We know what it is like to be the "odd one out" and have the wisdom to realize that it is through diversity that we achieve strength and tenacity. Our interviews revealed Witches are from all walks of life, adhering to a variety of religions and spiritual paths, and spanning the spectrum of sexuality and gender identity. Positive, life-affirming paths have been summarized to help you grasp the vast array of Witches in the world, and to give you the confidence to find your own path to walk. May your year be filled with many bright blessings!

This Year's Upgrades

Your weekly planner pages have been improved based on feedback from readers. The writing area for daily notes has been increased by 43% and days run vertically rather than tiled as they were in the past. Time zones are much easier to convert with a new map and a handy guide, making your almanac the perfect resource for any location on Earth. Data appearing in "small print" now incorporates a font that was specially designed to be legible in small sizes. This space-saving font allows us to provide more information and charted data.

In Varietate Concordia

Aloud we speak the names of the ancients;
dancing spirals under bright moonlit skies.
We walk our paths with courage and joy;
we are healers, scholars, seekers ~ the wise.

Content with the gold sun and silver moon;
no leaders or followers will you find;
for we know true power comes from within;
every Witch has an independent mind.

We celebrate our diverse traditions;
all paths are one and lead to the center.
United in perfect love and trust;
bright blessings and peace to all who enter.

~Friday Gladheart, 1996

This poem is an attempt to express the essence of what it means to be a Witch. It leans towards Paganism, but it has been used by Witches of many paths. You will find it in songs, invocations, book blessings and more, but until now the entire version and the title has never been published. The title is a Latin phrase meaning "unity in diversity" and its deeper meaning for Witches is that of unity without persecution, conformity, or uniformity; and diversity without segregation or fragmentation. This phrase comes to us from numerous ancient schools of thought and has been embraced by many people as a motto.

Key to Symbols

Moon Phases: ◖ 1st Quarter ○ Full ◗ 3rd Quarter ● New

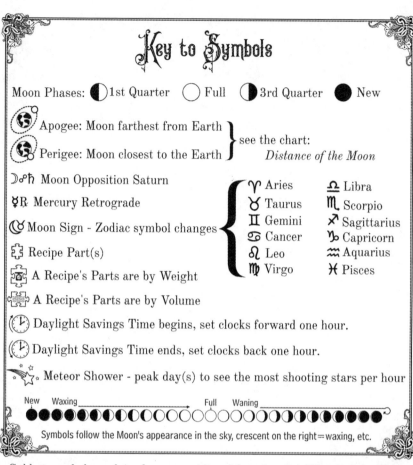

Apogee: Moon farthest from Earth ⎫
Perigee: Moon closest to the Earth ⎬ see the chart: *Distance of the Moon*
⎭

☽☍♄ Moon Opposition Saturn

☿℞ Mercury Retrograde

☾☿ Moon Sign - Zodiac symbol changes ⎰

⎱

♈ Aries   ♎ Libra
♉ Taurus   ♏ Scorpio
♊ Gemini   ♐ Sagittarius
♋ Cancer   ♑ Capricorn
♌ Leo   ♒ Aquarius
♍ Virgo   ♓ Pisces

Recipe Part(s)

A Recipe's Parts are by Weight

A Recipe's Parts are by Volume

Daylight Savings Time begins, set clocks forward one hour.

Daylight Savings Time ends, set clocks back one hour.

Meteor Shower - peak day(s) to see the most shooting stars per hour

New Waxing ———————————→ Full Waning ———————————

Symbols follow the Moon's appearance in the sky, crescent on the right = waxing, etc.

Sabbat symbols explained on page 42 and found on the Wheel of the Year.

Leap Year

February has 29 days this year because 2020 is a leap year. As you know, our calendars have 365 days. It takes the Earth 365 days plus 5 hours and 48+ minutes to travel around the sun. Every four years or so we add an extra day to our calendars so that we stay more in tune with this natural cycle. If we didn't do this, February and March would be warm summer months within just a few generations!

LEAP YEAR

Using Your Almanac

All astronomical events noted herein can be seen with the naked eye or simple binoculars. Experiencing these events deepens the understanding of both astronomy and astrology. It is one thing to see a bunch of symbols such as ☽♂♀ but the descriptions included here present you a sense of what these symbols mean and how to experience such events with full insights such as- *Conjunction of the Moon and Venus, see these two get together on your eastern horizon just after dusk.*

-48- Summaries of interviews with Witches are woven throughout your almanac with a cauldron symbol indicating the page numbers where they continue. At first glance, it may seem that these individuals have very little in common with each other. You may not resonate with every summary, but by identifying your personal differences and similarities you progress in forging your own path. It is our very differences that emphasize how being a Witch is such an individual journey of personal growth and discovery while being an inclusive path where anyone can find a niche. Our differences make us stronger and are celebrated. Despite our many unique paths, Witches have much in common: Independence, inner strength, strong wills, adventurous spirits, the urge to never take things at face value, and a knowledge of a vast array of disciplines considered by some to be "alternative" such as herbalism, healing with natural energies, divination, and magic.

Pages on the <u>left</u> side of your almanac contain articles, spells, recipes, monthly reviews, correspondences, and interview summaries.

These left side pages are designed to be long-term references for you to use for many years to come.

Pages on the <u>right</u> side have one-week-per-page planner pages for your schedule, goals, and events. At the top of each week's page is the week's number[2] corresponding to the **Weekly Index**. Under the week's number is a psychic insight for your consideration.

My Path

When a new month begins, the page opposite to the first week has a **My Path** section. This area helps you work harmoniously with the natural energy of the Moon to achieve your personal goals. Next to each month's date is an image of the corresponding Moon phase and marks indicating Waning, New, Waxing, and Full. For the purposes of energy work, anything over 97% is considered Full, and 3% or under is considered New. This prevents any confusion for those who walk paths that separate the New and Dark phases.[3] See **Working With the Moon** to learn how Moon phases can help you achieve your goals.

Walking Your Path

At the bottom of each month's **My Path** page is an area entitled *Walking Your Path*. It is designed to help you develop your skills to forge your own path with study prompts. If you wish to follow along these study prompts you will deepen your understanding of several disciplines whether you are just beginning your studies or have been practicing for many turns of the Wheel of the Year. These prompts correspond to the Directories that begin on page 112. You may enjoy exploring these prompts as casually or intensely as you like.

Herbalism

Three herbs are featured each month with common names listed in your monthly review. Use the **Herb Directory** in the back of your almanac to find the botanical binomials[4] (a.k.a. *"Latin names"* or *"scientific names"*) for the common names. All names have power, and by using the proper binomial for an herb you can speed up your research and prevent mistakes. Becoming proficient in herbalism requires that you learn a bit of Latin and Greek, but you may find out that it is a thrill to discover the history of plant names and some of the interesting stories of how they came to be. The article *Decoding the Binomials* on page 94 will help make this adventure easy and fun. The pronunciation of a few of the trickier genus and common names are included in the Herbal Directory so that you sound like an expert[*] and will know how to properly say patchouli (did someone sneeze?).

The Energies of Stones

Three stones are listed each month and correspond to the **Stones, Crystals & Minerals Directory**. Even if you only have a casual interest in this area, you may find yourself incorporating some of these natural materials into your path. These tools can enrich your life every day.

Divinatory Arts

Tarot: From January through November, two Major Arcana tarot cards are featured on the My Path page as study prompts. Refer to your **Tarot Directory** to expand your list of associated keywords. On Sundays in your planner pages, a Minor Arcana tarot card is noted, with two cards appearing on the last three weeks in December.

The Moon

Runes: Two runes are featured each month. Runes are rich in meaning, history, and use. Your **Rune Directory** may be just the beginning of your studies if you discover that this path calls to you.

Consider Before Casting

This unique section contains things to think about to help you learn more about yourself and the use of your energy in magic and the mundane world. You might also be inspired to use these as seed ideas and questions for discussion groups, journaling or a Book of Shadows.

---

[*]   The pronunciations provided correspond to those used in the Americas but don't worry, Brittish and other regional pronunciations vary only slightly.

All Tarot Cards in your almanac are renditions adapted from Pamela Coleman Smith's designs used in the 1909 Rider-Waite tarot deck. Smith's work set a standard of symbolism now used in many decks.

Simpler's Method & Recipe Symbols

Apothecary style recipes are provided using the traditional "simpler's method"[5] that relies on the flexibility of "parts". A part can be a measurement of weight _or_ volume. At the top of a recipe, you will see a puzzle piece with **waves for volume**, or a **scale for weight**. The parts in the recipe are then noted as a small puzzle piece.

For this first blessing incense, the puzzle piece at the top indicates volume. If you wish to make a small amount, you could use a teaspoon (tsp.) as each part. You would then use 3 tsp. sandalwood, 1 tsp. copal and 1 tsp. cinnamon. For a large batch, you might use a tablespoon for your "parts".

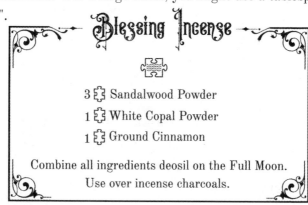

Blessing Incense

3 Sandalwood Powder

1 White Copal Powder

1 Ground Cinnamon

Combine all ingredients deosil on the Full Moon.
Use over incense charcoals.

This next recipe is _parts by weight_ (with a scale puzzle piece). You might try a tiny batch using a gram as your part, or a large batch by using an ounce part.

Blessing Incense

6 Sandalwood Chips (small)

1 White Copal Granules

1 Gum Mastic Granules

Combine all ingredients deosil on the Full Moon.
Use over incense charcoals.

Almanac Time

The almanac you hold in your hands is uniquely suited to help you view astronomical occurrences, plan energy and magical work according to moon phases, coordinate online rituals to coincide with Sabbats, and for calculating astrological events. This is due to the consistent use of a single time zone for all data, Central Time. Daylight Savings Time (DST) is already accounted for in the U.S., and you do not need to add an hour from March 8 to November 1.

Annuals such as almanacs and calendars do not often state the time zone used. Most are set for Greenwich Mean Time (GMT), with Eastern Time coming in a close second place. To make things more difficult, some events will be listed in Eastern, while moon phases are listed in GMT. A large majority of annual guides do not inform you when DST is in effect, or if it has even been calculated into the data. That is a big problem when you are trying to see the peak of an eclipse, only to find that your calendar instructed you to attempt viewing an hour too early, or worse yet, too late. Timing rituals can also be problematic.

The data for all annual guides such as almanacs is "fitted" to a specific location, meaning that all calculations are based on that one place. Usually, this is the Royal Observatory in Greenwich (GMT) and all data is simply calculated with an hourly offset such as subtracting six hours to get Central Time. The Practical Witch's Almanac is set for Central Time and is fitted to W 93° 21', N 34° 35' as indicated by the pin on the map on the next page. Central Time is easier to convert to most time zones in North and South America than GMT, and it covers a large area of the United States, Canada, and Mexico.

The pin on the map is the location of the PaganPath.com Sanctuary, home of the oldest online academy for practical magic, Witchcraft, Wicca, herbalism, tarot, and other divination arts.

A tree is planted at this sanctuary for every printed almanac sold.

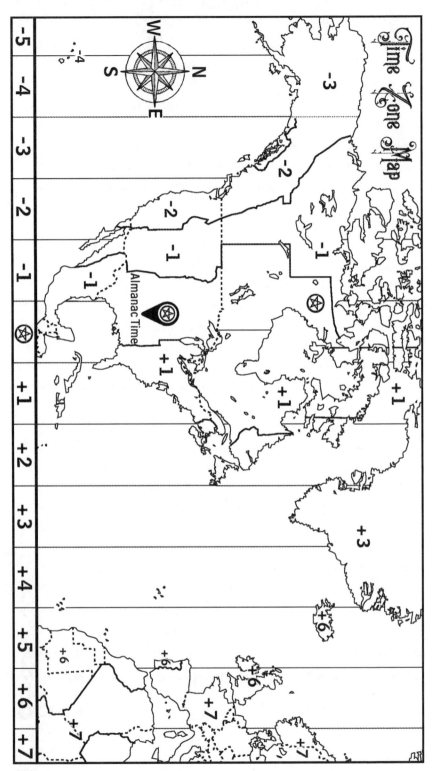

Time Zone Conversions

When the map on the opposite page does not show your area, you can go to the PracticalWitch.com website to convert any time, or to look up your "offset". Below is a list of common offsets for major areas. Add or subtract as indicated based on the city that shares your time zone.

Auckland, New Zealand +19	Amsterdam, Netherlands +7
New Plymouth, New Zealand +19	Madrid, Spain +7
Sydney, Australia +17	Rome, Italy +7
Melbourne, Australia +17	Dublin, Ireland +6
Cairns, Australia +16	Lisbon, Portugal +6
Adelaide, Australia +16.5	Prague, Czech Republic +6
Alice Springs, Australia +15.5	Reykjavik, Iceland +6
Tokyo, Japan +15	Glasgow, United Kingdom +6
Perth, Australia +14	Ittoqqortoormiit, Greenland +5
Shanghai, China +14	Nuuk, Greenland +3
Hong Kong, China +14	Halifax, Canada +2
New Delhi, India +11.5	Bridgetown, Barbados +2
Moscow, Russia +9	Nassau, Bahamas +1
Cairo, Egypt +8	Ottawa, Canada +1
Athens, Greece +8	Port-au-Prince, Haiti +1
Rovaniemi, Finland +8	New York, NY, USA +1
Paris, France +7	Denver, CO, USA -1
Longyearbyen, Norway +7	Portland, OR, USA -2
Zürich, Switzerland +7	Phoenix, AZ, USA -1 (Mar. 8th-Nov. 1st: -2)
Berlin, Germany +7	Honolulu, HI, USA -4
Chicago, IL, USA - same as almanac	Omaha, NE, USA - same as almanac

A few areas do not observe DST (e.g. most of Arizona except the Navajo Nation and the North-East corner): Subtract an extra hour from Almanac Time Mar. 8 to Nov. 1.

My Path

Waxing	) 1	_____
	) 2	_____
	◖ 3	_____
	◖ 4	_____
	◖ 5	_____
	◖ 6	_____
	◯ 7	_____
	◯ 8	_____

Full	◯ 9	_____
	◯10	_____
	◯11	_____
	◯12	_____

Waning	◯13	_____
	◯14	_____
	◖15	_____
	◖16	_____
	◖17	_____
	(18	_____
	(19	_____
	(20	_____
	ı 21	_____
	ı 22	_____

New	23	_____
	24	_____
	25	_____
	ı26	_____

Waxing	ı27	_____
	)28	_____
	)29	_____
	)30	_____
	◖31	_____

January

Week	Mo	Tu	We	Th	Fr	Sa	Su
1			1	2	3	4	5
2	6	7	8	9	10	11	12
3	13	14	15	16	17	18	19
4	20	21	22	23	24	25	26
5	27	28	29	30	31		

2 ◑   10 ◯   17 ◐   24 ●

January is National Blood Donor Month, National Braille Literacy Month, National Hobby Month, and Hot Tea Month.

⊗ Walking Your Path ⬦

Herbalism Study: Rosemary, Sage, Wormwood
Stones to Study: Rose Quartz, Tourmaline, Jasper
Consider before Casting: Sometimes the best thing you can do to help others and yourself is to love both.

THE FOOL .

THE MAGICIAN .

Often thought to be named after the Roman God Janus, this month's name actually comes from the Latin ianua, meaning door.

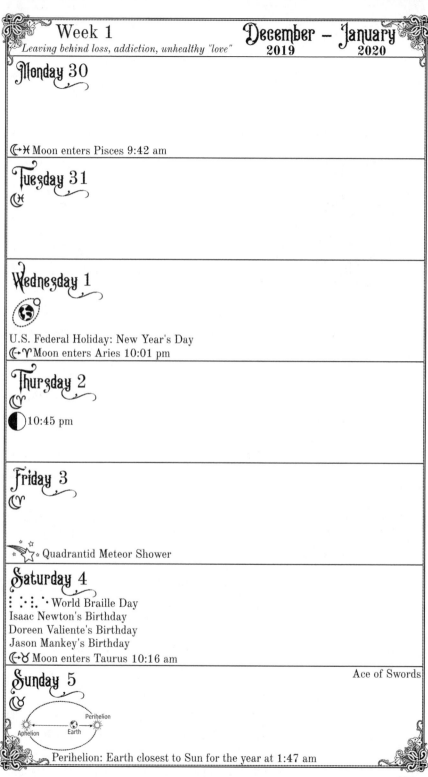

Monday 30

☾→♓ Moon enters Pisces 9:42 am

Tuesday 31
☾♓

Wednesday 1

U.S. Federal Holiday: New Year's Day
☾→♈ Moon enters Aries 10:01 pm

Thursday 2
☾♈

◐ 10:45 pm

Friday 3
☾♈

☆ Quadrantid Meteor Shower

Saturday 4

World Braille Day
Isaac Newton's Birthday
Doreen Valiente's Birthday
Jason Mankey's Birthday
☾→♉ Moon enters Taurus 10:16 am

Sunday 5
☾♉

Ace of Swords

Perihelion: Earth closest to Sun for the year at 1:47 am

What are You Fishing For?

As calculations are made during the creation of your almanac, it becomes clear that there are certain times that are well suited to specific activities.

Lunar and solar forces coincide with subtle astrological and magical energies to increase the likelihood of success in many endeavors.

The dates below are good fishing times. They are also excellent days to **attract or draw things toward you** such as **finding magical and spiritual tools in nature.** If you are looking for a wand in the woods or a stone or crystal, these days will be particularly fortuitous. Hunting for crystals will be easier on these days, especially after recent rains and near the Full and New Moon phases.

In general, these are days of **prosperity, opportunities, fertility, strength, and good luck.** These are also good days for **travel, finding lost objects, and hunting.**[*]

January: 10, 11, 12, 13	**July:** 4, 5, 25
February: 8, 9, 10	**August:** 3, 4, 20, 21
March: 8, 9, 10	**September:** 1, 2, 17, 18
April: 6, 7, 8 (especially 7th)	**October:** 1, 16, 17, 31
May: 5, 6, 7, 8	**November:** 13, 14, 29, 30
June: 3, 4, 5, 29	**December:** 12, 28, 29, 30

---

[*] Pictured: A stylized Hei Matau (pronounced hay mah-Tah-oo) or Maori fish hook. The Pagan Maori of New Zealand carve pendants and create tattoos of this design for prosperity, fertility, strength, good luck, abundance, prestige, power, good health, authority, and safe passage over water.

Monday 6

☾→♊ Moon enters Gemini 8:11 pm

Tuesday 7
☾♊

Wednesday 8
☾♊

Thursday 9

☾→♋ Moon enters Cancer 2:44 am

Friday 10
☾♋

Penumbral Lunar Eclipse

○ 1:21 pm

☽☍♄ 5:43 pm

Saturday 11

☾→♌ Moon enters Leo 6:16 am

Ace of Wands

Sunday 12
☾♌

Working With the Moon

Changing your perspective of a mundane or magical challenge can help you be more successful in achieving your goals. Changing your approach is easier when you work harmoniously with the natural energies of the Moon. The corporate slogan "think outside the box" is not just a poster in an office cubicle or board room, it is a valid technique for unveiling solutions.

The My Path section found at the beginning of each month in the planner pages shows the Moon illumination[*] marked alongside a list of dates. The phases of the moon are marked next to this, and you can use this guide to help you shift your approach to your projects.

Waxing ●●●●●●●○○

During the Waxing phase, the bright crescent appears on the right side of the Moon and increases (waxes) in size as the days pass to the Full Moon. This is a time of putting your plans into action and laying the foundations of new projects. It is usually a very productive time to get the ball rolling towards achieving your goals. As with the light of the Moon, this phase is all about growth.

Keywords: Action, Gaining, Increasing, Energy, Attraction, Creativity, Strength, Building, Motivation, Germination, Manifestation, Growth, Drawing

Full ○○○

A very magical time to reap the "seeds" you planted in the New phase and grew in the Waxing phase. It is a time of abundance, intuition, achievement, and power. The results of your work have manifest or are manifesting. This is a time of high energy that crackles with magic. Because of this, it is not necessarily the best time for making

---

[*] See page 127 for a complete chart of the actual Illumination of the Moon for all dates in 2020.

Monday 13

☾→♍ Moon enters Virgo 8:07 am

Tuesday 14
☾♍

Wednesday 15

☾→♎ Moon enters Libra 9:44 am

Thursday 16
☾♎

Friday 17

● 6:58 am
☾→♏ Moon enters Scorpio 12:21 pm

Saturday 18
☾♏

Sunday 19

Ace of Cups

☾♏

World Religions Day
☾→♐ Moon enters Sagittarius 4:41 pm

plans and choices. It is a fantastic time to use the intense power of the Moon to work on the plans you have already made, and to really bring those plans into the physical world.

Keywords: Celebration, Manifestation, Acts of Love and Pleasure, Magic, Intuition, Psychicism

Waning

As the light crescent of the moon swings to the left, we are reminded that this is a time of letting go and release. It is a good time to break baneful habits or patterns to make room for better things. This is the perfect time for housekeeping on many levels - magically, mentally, and materially.

Keywords: Banishing, Release, Undoing, Reverse, Sending Away, Reflection, Overcoming Obstacles, Introspection, Cleansing

New & Dark³ ●●●

This phase is a good time for planning, resting, and begin grateful. It is also a great time for fresh starts, planting seeds, new projects, and beginnings, especially after the date of the actual New Moon. Although divination is always useful, it can be particularly helpful during this phase to help reflect, release, and plan.

Keywords: Regeneration, Plant, Gratitude, New Beginnings, Dreaming, Spa Days, Fresh Starts, Strategize, Refresh, Release, Peace, Introspection, Planting, Transformation, Recuperation

 From here we cycle back around to the Waxing phase. Some practitioners simply work with two major phases for spellwork: Waxing/Full and Waning/New. You can see by reviewing the attributes and energy of these combinations that those phase pairings are complimentary. You might try the two phases at first and refine to the four or vice versa, your path is yours to forge.

Monday 20

U.S. Federal Holiday:
  Martin Luther King Jr. Day
Moon close to Mars on the eastern
  horizon before sunrise
☼→♒ Sun enters Aquarius 8:55 am

Tuesday 21

☾→♑ Moon enters Capricorn 11:00 pm

Wednesday 22
♑

Thursday 23
♑

Friday 24

● 3:42 pm
☾→♒ Moon enters Aquarius 7:21 am

Saturday 25
♒

Chinese New Year: Year of the White Metal Rat

Ace of Pentacles

Sunday 26

☾→♓ Moon enters Pisces 5:44 pm

My Path

	) 1 ☉	
Waxing	◑ 2 ☉	
	◑ 3	
	◑ 4 ☉	
	◑ 5	
	◑ 6	
	◑ 7	
Full	◑ 8	
	◯ 9	
	◯ 10	
Waning	◯ 11	
	◯ 12	
	◯ 13	
	◑ 14	
	◑ 15	
	◑ 16	
	(17	
	(18	
	(19	
	(20	
New	21	
	22	
	23	
	24	
	) 25	
Waxing	) 26	
	) 27	
	) 28	
	) 29	

Week	Mo	Tu	We	Th	Fr	Sa	Su
5						1	2
6	3	4	5	6	7	8	9
7	10	11	12	13	14	15	16
8	17	18	19	20	21	22	23
9	24	25	26	27	28	29	

1 ◑   9 ◯   15 ◑   23 ●

February is Black History Month (U.S. & Canada), LGBT History Month (UK), American Heart Month, and Great American Pie Month.

Ⓕ Walking Your Path Ⓑ

Herbalism Study: Lavender, Patchouli, Thyme
Stones to Study: Red Tiger Eye, Selenite, Unakite
Consider before Casting: Timing, Tools, Focus, Intent - these help to direct Your Will.

The Cimaruta (pronounced chee-mah-rroó-tah) is a very old protection charm that resembles a branch of the Rue plant. It is a composite charm, meaning it is made from more than one charm, and is popular with Stregheria.

Monday 27
☽♓

World Holocaust Victims Remembrance Day

Tuesday 28
☽♓

See the Moon and Venus on their way to conjunction
near the south-west horizon at dusk

Wednesday 29

Oprah Winfrey's Birthday
☽→♈ Moon enters Aries 5:51 am

Thursday 30
☽♈

Z. Budapest's Birthday

Friday 31

☽→♉ Moon enters Taurus 6:28 pm

Saturday 1
☽♉

◗ 7:41 pm
National Freedom Day

Sunday 2
☽♉

Two of Swords

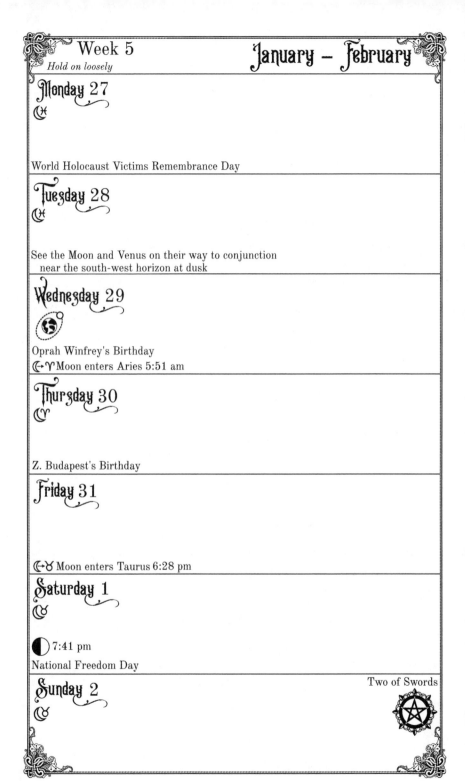

Sun & Moon in Zodiac Signs

When the Moon is Full, it is always in the Zodiac sign opposite the Sun. The New Moon is always in the same Zodiac sign as the Sun. In this illustration, consider December 2020 when the Sun is in Capricorn. This means that the New Moon for December will also be in Capricorn, and the Full Moon will be on the opposite side of the Zodiac in Cancer.

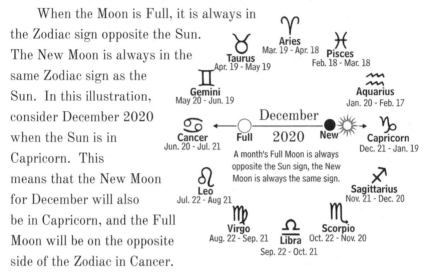

Aries Mar. 19 - Apr. 18
Pisces Feb. 18 - Mar. 18
Taurus Apr. 19 - May 19
Aquarius Jan. 20 - Feb. 17
Gemini May 20 - Jun. 19
December
Cancer Jun. 20 - Jul. 21
Full **2020** **New**
Capricorn Dec. 21 - Jan. 19
A month's Full Moon is always opposite the Sun sign, the New Moon is always the same sign.
Leo Jul. 22 - Aug 21
Sagittarius Nov. 21 - Dec. 20
Virgo Aug. 22 - Sep. 21
Scorpio Oct. 22 - Nov. 20
Libra Sep. 22 - Oct. 21

The energy of a Moon phase is thought to be influenced by its Zodiac sign. By working harmoniously with these energies, you may find it easier to accomplish your goals.

Aries: Work on short-term objectives and challenges, matters that require courage and inner strength. For example, combine the Moon in Aries with the New Moon (such as March 24, 2020) you have the perfect time to break negative addiction, habits, and patterns.

Taurus: Long-term objective for solid foundations. Peaceful relationships and cooperation, protection spells, artistic and creative endeavors.

Gemini: Thoughts and communication objectives. Divination is especially good at this time. Communication and education projects go well.

Cancer: Focus on home, security, comfort, and family. Cleanse and bless your home. Purification baths are wonderful at this time.

Leo: Creativity, taking risks, charisma, charity, physical fitness, confidence, passion, inspiration. Dare yourself to take on a new challenge.

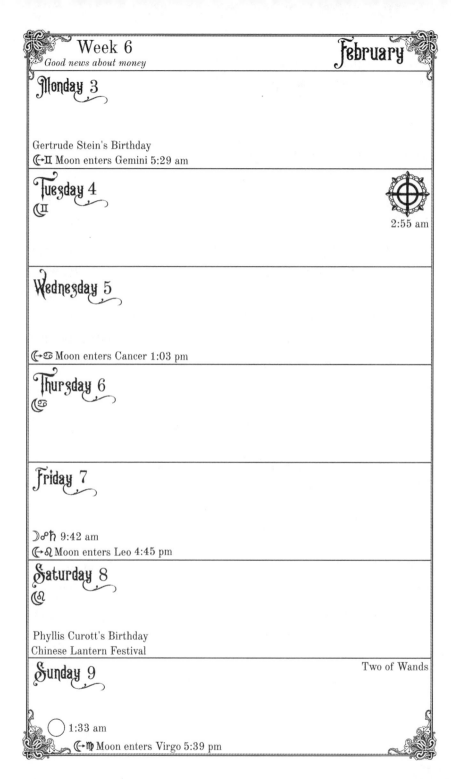

Monday 3

Gertrude Stein's Birthday
☾←Ⅱ Moon enters Gemini 5:29 am

Tuesday 4
☾Ⅱ

2:55 am

Wednesday 5

☾←♋ Moon enters Cancer 1:03 pm

Thursday 6
☾♋

Friday 7

☽☌♄ 9:42 am
☾←♌ Moon enters Leo 4:45 pm

Saturday 8
☾♌

Phyllis Curott's Birthday
Chinese Lantern Festival

Sunday 9

Two of Wands

◯ 1:33 am
☾←♍ Moon enters Virgo 5:39 pm

Virgo: Details, routines, healing, weight management, calculated tasks, health and domestic goals, consecrations, hearth and home.

Libra: Connections, cooperation, harmonious objectives, legal matters, contracts. This is a good Moon sign for business dealings.

Scorpio: Accounting for self and closing old accounts, protection and transformation spells, banishing, physical passion, and lust.

Sagittarius: Adventures, expanding horizons, education, magical studies, divination, travel, spirituality, intuition, and psychic skills.

Capricorn: Long term objectives, practical goals. Banishing, career success, improving status, building relationships, breaking ground.

Aquarius: Connections, new group objectives, focus on others, working toward the greater good, acquiring new technology (devices).

Pisces: Magical and spiritual objectives, creativity, astral work, divination, dream magic, psychic development, banishing negativity, finding lost objects, brewing, meditation.

Gardening by the Moon

Witches and permaculturists share an understanding that the practice of producing food, medicines, and energy must be performed sustainably. Both also share the objectives of working harmoniously with the resources and patterns all around us. Gardening 'by the Moon" helps to achieve these goals, and Witches enjoy the added energy of the appropriate moon phase when working with plants for magic. Garden tasks are done when the Moon is in certain signs.

Water Signs (Leaf) - Cancer, Pisces, Scorpio: Planting above-ground crops such as leafy herbs (Rosemary, Chives, Sage), cabbages, broccoli, spinach. This is a good time to deep-water the garden and trees.

Earth Signs (Root) - Taurus, Virgo, Capricorn: Plant underground crops to encourage root and underground stem growth (potatoes, mandrake, ginseng, carrots, Jerusalem artichokes). Capricorn is especially

Monday 10
♑

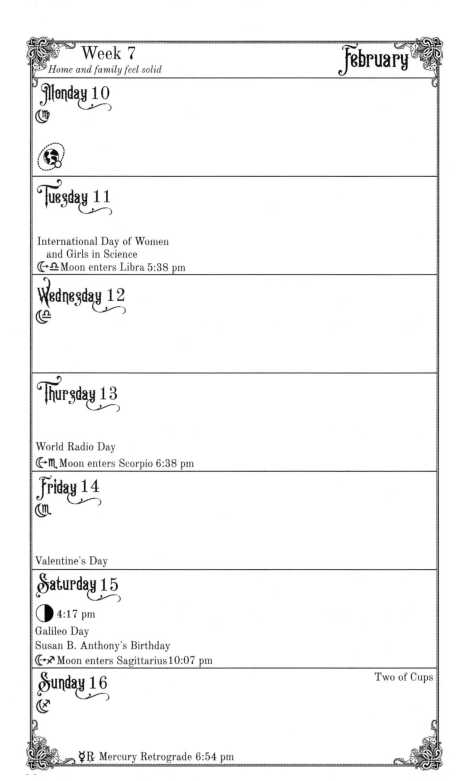

Tuesday 11

International Day of Women
 and Girls in Science
☾→♎ Moon enters Libra 5:38 pm

Wednesday 12
☾♎

Thursday 13

World Radio Day
☾→♏ Moon enters Scorpio 6:38 pm

Friday 14
☾♏

Valentine's Day

Saturday 15

◖ 4:17 pm
Galileo Day
Susan B. Anthony's Birthday
☾→♐ Moon enters Sagittarius 10:07 pm

Sunday 16
☾♐

Two of Cups

☿℞ Mercury Retrograde 6:54 pm

noted for being a good time to plant root crops. The Earth signs are also great for inoculating with mycorrhizal spores and beneficial nematodes. Transplant in these times while root growth is accentuated.

Air Signs (Flower) - Libra, Gemini, Aquarius: Harvest, weed, cultivate. When the Moon is in Libra you may find that planting herbs that are grown for their flowers is more successful. Chamomile, elder, rose petals, and calendula are good examples of flower crops.

Fire Signs (Fruit & Seed) - Aries, Leo, Sagittarius: Prune and weed, harvest and preserve. Drying herbs may be faster and easier.

Looking for just the right day to plant? Check the days in your Almanac during the waxing moon and plant in a Water or Earth sign.

Trying to keep the weeds down or harvest and dry some herbs? Check the days during the Waning Moon and pick a day when the Moon is in a Fire or Air sign.

There are exceptions to this general guide. Witches sometimes harvest plants for spellwork involving increase during the Waxing or Full Moon, and plants for banishing during the Waning or New Moon. When in doubt, harvesting on the Full Moon is the "default" and adds a bit of energy to the herbs that can be utilized for any type of working.

Perigee: In the gardens at the Pagan sanctuary where your Almanac is created, we have discovered that when the Moon is at Perigee, seeds seem to sprout better and herbs have a slightly higher essential oil content. For this reason, we harvest many herbs and plants for magic, medicine, and food during "Supermoons" when possible and practical.

Moon Opposition Saturn ☽☍♄

The dates that the Moon is opposite Saturn are marked in your almanac. These are excellent times to use mycorrhizal spores, beneficial nematodes, and plant seeds. Biodynamic gardeners use sprays at this time to increase the beneficial microbial activity in the soil.

Monday 17
☾♐

U.S. Federal Holiday: Presidents Day

Tuesday 18

Look to the south-eastern horizon before
    dawn to see Moon-Mars conjunction
☀→♓ Sun enters Pisces 10:57 pm
☾→♑ Moon enters Capricorn 4:37 am

Wednesday 19
☾♑

Catch Moon and Jupiter nearing conjunction
    before dawn on the south-eastern horizon
Nicolaus Copernicus's Birthday

Thursday 20

Look west along the horizon after sunset
    to see Moon and Venus conjunction
World Day of Social Justice
☾→♒ Moon enters Aquarius 1:42pm

Friday 21
☾♒

Barbara Jordan's Birthday

Saturday 22
☾♒

Sybil Leek's Birthday

Sunday 23

Two of Pentacles

 9:32 am
    ☾→♓ Moon enters Pisces 12:38 am

My Path

Waxing

*)1
● 2
● 3
● 4
○ 5
○ 6
○ 7

Full

○ 8
○ 9
○10

Waning

○11
○12
○13
○14
○15
● 16
(17
(18
(19 ⚙
(20
21
22

23
24
25
26

Waxing

)27
)28
)29
● 30
● 31

		March					
Week	Mo	Tu	We	Th	Fr	Sa	Su
9							1
10	2	3	4	5	6	7	8
11	9	10	11	12	13	14	15
12	16	17	18	**19**	20	21	22
13	23	24	25	26	27	28	29
14	30	31					

2 ◐   9 ○   16 ◑   24 ●

March is National Women's History Month, Social Workers Month, National Craft Month, and National Irish American Heritage Month.

Ⓜ Walking Your Path Ⓕ

Herbalism Study: Rose, Dill, Chives
Stones to Study: Wavellite, Sodalite, Rhodonite
Consider before Casting: Imagine meeting your past-self. What advice would you give yourself to help you meet the challenges you face today?

A tissane is a tea of flowers, bark, berries, leaves, roots, or seeds that does not have Camellia sinensis (the true tea plant). Pronounced like tea's on (teé-zon).

Monday 24
☾ ♓

Tuesday 25

☾→♈ Moon enters Aries 12:48 pm

Wednesday 26
☾ ♈

Thursday 27
☾ ♈

Friday 28

☾→♉ Moon enters Taurus 1:30 am

Saturday 29
☾ ♉

Sunday 1   Three of Swords

Zero Discrimination Day
☾→♊ Moon enters Gemini 1:21 pm

Dark Moons & New Moons

Cast ye this spell on the dark of the Moon,
gather white oak then engrave this rune. . .

Many spells instruct you to cast during the "Dark of the Moon". There are three main approaches to working with the Dark Moon. Before delving into these approaches, consider that the data provided in your almanac for a specific phase such as Full or New is a very brief moment in time.

When transitioning phases, the Moon is in a **liminal** state. Liminality is another way of saying "between the worlds" or "betwixt and between". Witches are familiar with "tweens", as we walk between the mundane and magical worlds on a daily basis. Your **My Path** section at the beginning of each month gives you a visual overview of the Moon's constant flux and liminal phases. With this visual, you can take any one of the three approaches to the Dark of the Moon that you prefer.

New Moons
January ♒
24th - 3:42 pm
February ♓
23rd - 9:32 am
March ♈
24th - 4:28 am
April ♉
22nd - 9:25 pm
May ♊
22nd - 12:38 pm
June ♋
21st - 1:41 am
July ♋
20th - 12:32 pm
August ♌
18th - 9:41 pm
September ♍
17th - 6:00 am
October ♎
16th - 2:31 pm
November ♏
14th - 11:07 pm
December ♐
14th - 10:16 pm

The Dark Moon as a liminal phase. The New Moon is a specific moment in time during this liminal phase. You can get a feel for this when you consider certain initiatory groups where a new candidate goes through a rite of passage known as an Initiation. During this ritual, the initiate experiences a liminal phase when she is no longer a candidate and not yet a priestess. The ritual is a single moment, but initiation is a liminal phase that one experiences over a longer period of time, both before and after the actual rite of passage.

Of the three approaches the first two account for less than 15% of people we interviewed for the almanac, with the remaining 85% or more using the more traditional third approach.

Monday 2
♑ ♊

◗ 1:57 pm

Tuesday 3

World Wildlife Day
National Academy of Sciences founded 1863
☾→♋ Moon enters Cancer 10:25 pm

Wednesday 4
☾ ♋

Thursday 5
☾ ♋

Friday 6

☽☌♄ 1:11 am
☾→♌ Moon enters Leo 3:28 am

Saturday 7
☾ ♌

Sunday 8

Three of Wands

🕐 Clocks +1 hour (U.S.) at 2:00 am
International Women's Day
☾→♍ Moon enters Virgo 5:47 am

First Approach

Recently, a few books on introductory magic and Wicca have modified the traditional definitions of New Moon and Dark Moon in this new approach. This has caused a bit of confusion as practitioners who follow these new teachings publish spells and articles with the New Moon separate from the Dark Moon, leaving traditional practitioners uncertain of the spell's timing. These traditions refer to the Dark Moon as the three days prior to the New Moon. Adherents refrain from doing any magic at this time (labeling it "Hecate's rule"). This recent "rule" is not such a bad idea, particularly for new practitioners who tend to sling spells on a daily basis in their enthusiasm.

Second Approach

For this approach, the Dark Moon refers to the last visible crescent of the Moon and continues until the New Moon. This is similar to the third approach. However, in these traditions, the New Moon is considered to be the first visible crescent Moon instead of the scientific event.

Third Approach

In most traditions, the Dark Moon is the time when the Moon cannot be seen in the sky, usually for about three days. This allocation has a considerably longer historical, magical, maritime, and scientific basis. These three days include the day of the actual New Moon, the exactly timed astrological occurrence when the Moon is entirely in the umbra (shadow) of the Earth. This single moment is like our initiate's rite of passage, an exact time during a longer liminal phase. In much the same way that we approach the Full Moon phase for magic, the New Moon is both a single moment and a state of liminality lasting a few days. Dark Moon is used interchangeably with New Moon for magical purposes, and for more exact timing the New Moon data is used to pinpoint the peak of the Moon's energy during this liminal phase.

Monday 9
☾♍

◯ "Supermoon" 12:47 pm
☿ Mercury Direct 10:49 pm

Tuesday 10
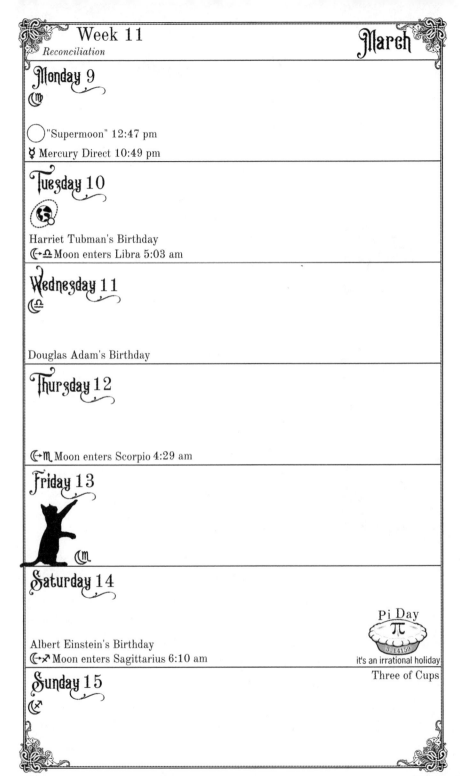

Harriet Tubman's Birthday
☾→♎ Moon enters Libra 5:03 am

Wednesday 11
☾♎

Douglas Adam's Birthday

Thursday 12

☾→♏ Moon enters Scorpio 4:29 am

Friday 13

☾♏

Saturday 14

Albert Einstein's Birthday
☾→♐ Moon enters Sagittarius 6:10 am

Pi Day
π
3.14159
it's an irrational holiday

Three of Cups

Sunday 15
☾♐

Sabbats & Symbols

The names of holidays and holy days vary by tradition, and your path might not include all eight Sabbats. No matter what you call the or which you celebrate, the precise dates of the Quarters and Cross-Quarters are marked in your almanac with an eight-spoked wheel. The different symbols within this eight-spoked wheel indicate...

Cross-Quarters or "Greater" Sabbats: These Sabba are said to be older, with a long history of celebratio over many regions. They are not necessarily more important. However, Beltane and Samhain are cele-brated by the majority of Witches.

Quarters or "Lesser" Sabbats: These solar based Sabbats are the Equinoxes and Solstices of the year. There are two Solstices and two Equinoxes.

Exact Cross-Quarters: The traditional Sabbats or Cross-Quarters fall about halfway between the Equinoxes and Solstices, and again from Solstices to Equinoxes, etc. Over time, calendars have changed and astronomical measurements have advanced.

Rather than simply counting the days between a Quarter Sabbat and dividing in half (subject to the fallibility of clocks and calendars), your almanac uses the very precise method based on the position of the Sun and the tilt of the Earth. Exact Cross-Quarter are when the Sun reaches a precisely 45-degree arc along the ecliptic between the Quarters (which are 90 degrees apart). Unlike secular holidays that begin and end at midnight and are dictated by commerci marketing, Sabbats are often celebrated over a longer period of time. Most Witches begin the festivities on the evening before the traditiona

Monday 16

 4:34 am
 Moon enters Capricorn 11:26 am

Tuesday 17
♑

○ St. Patrick's Day

Wednesday 18

Rise before dawn to see the conjunctions of
the Moon and Mars, Jupiter, and Saturn
on the south-eastern horizon. Wow!

☾→♒ Moon enters Aquarius 8:16 pm

Thursday 19
♒

10:50 pm

☀→♈ Sun enters Aries 10:50 pm

Friday 20
♒

Jupiter and Mars can be seen on the south-eastern
horizon just before dawn as they reach conjunction
International Day of Happiness

Saturday 21

World Poetry Day
World Day to Eliminate Racial Discrimination
International Day of Forests

☾→♓ Moon enters Pisces 7:34 am

Three of Pentacles

Sunday 22
♓

 World Water Day

date and continue until the day after the Exact Cross-Quarter. Celebrations on the Cross-Quarter Sabbats are often held over a longer period of time than Quarter Sabbats.

This precise spacial method of calculating the Exact Cross-Quarters by interpolating the mid-points between Solstices and Equinoxes as measured along the ecliptic was established in the mid-1980s by former NASA scientist Rollin Gillespie. This data can now be found in many places, but we tip our pointy hats to the archaeoastronomy.com website in gratitude for being the first and best to provide this information to the public early on in the beginning days of the internet.

The Path of the Southern Hemisphere Witch

The inside front cover displays a Wheel of the Year for the Northern Hemisphere (NH). The back cover displays the Southern Hemisphere's (SH) Wheel. Which Sabbats you celebrate at what time of the year is entirely up to you but, this is how other "south paws" proceed:

Some SH Witches follow the traditional NH Wheel, celebrating Samhain in October as do most U.K. and U.S. traditions. However, it can be difficult to prepare for this "harvest" Sabbat when it is early spring outside your door, and the season in the SH in October is that of Beltane in the NH. For some SH Witches, it makes sense to work harmoniously with the cycles of nature, celebrating the Sabbats according to the actual season.

Many SH initiates will begin their practice by following the NH Wheel because that is what their NH traditions and books teach. This works quite well for some, but for others, it makes it difficult to attune to the seasonal energy of the Sabbat. Those who fall into the later group usually change to the SH Wheel once they move from studying into practice.

Sub rosa is Latin for "under the rose." The use of this phrase has a very long history and it indicates secrecy and confidentiality. What happens at a sub rosa meeting stays at the sub rosa meeting.

♏ Monday 23

☾→♈ Moon enters Aries 7:59 pm

♉ Tuesday 24
☾♈

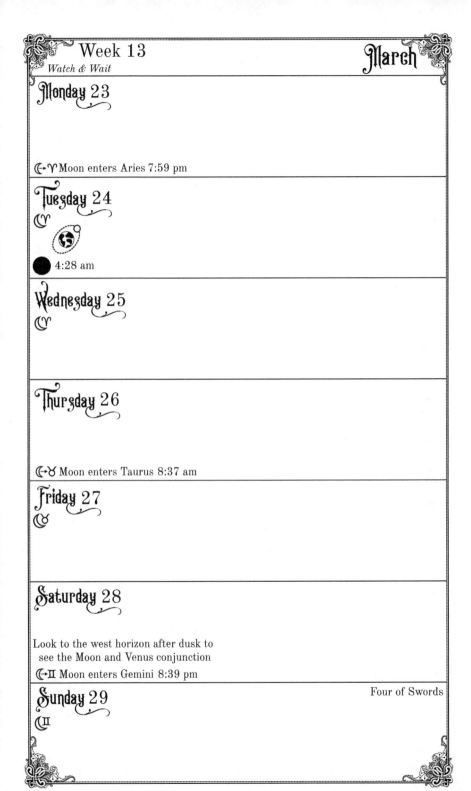

● 4:28 am

♈ Wednesday 25
☾♈

♈ Thursday 26

☾→♉ Moon enters Taurus 8:37 am

♉ Friday 27
☾♉

♊ Saturday 28

Look to the west horizon after dusk to
see the Moon and Venus conjunction
☾→♊ Moon enters Gemini 8:39 pm

♊ Sunday 29   Four of Swords
☾♊

My Path

Waxing
- ◐ 1 *
- ◑ 2
- ◐ 3
- ◐ 4
- ◐ 5
- ◐ 6

Full
- ◯ 7
- ◯ 8
- ◯ 9

Waning
- ◑ 10
- ◑ 11
- ◑ 12
- ◑ 13
- ◑ 14
- ◖ 15
- ◖ 16
- ◖ 17
- ◖ 18
- ◗ 19
- ◗ 20

New
- ◗ 21
- ◗ 22
- ◗ 23
- ◗ 24

Waxing
- ◗ 25
- ◗ 26
- ◗ 27
- ◗ 28
- ◐ 29
- ◐ 30 ✿

April

Week	Mo	Tu	We	Th	Fr	Sa	Su
14			1	2	3	4	5
15	6	7	8	9	10	11	12
16	13	14	15	16	17	18	19
17	20	21	22	23	24	25	26
18	27	28	29	**30**			

1 ◑ 7 ◯ 14 ◑ 22 ● 30 ◑

April is National Child Abuse Prevention Month, National Poetry Month, National Autism Awareness Month, National Volunteer Month, National Humor Month, and Sexual Assault Awareness Month.

Ⓝ Walking Your Path Ⓢ

Herbalism Study: Oregano, Marjoram, Cinquefoil

Stones to Study: Snowflake Obsidian, Selenite, Malachite

Consider before Casting: How does my daily routine enrich my spiritual life and bring me closer to my goals?

A three-ring binder or scrapbook with removable pages makes a great magical Journal or Book of Shadows (BoS). Decorative page templates for your BoS can be found at PracticalWitch.com

Monday 30
☾♊

Tuesday 31
Conjunction of Saturn & Mars can be seen
  just before dawn on the south-eastern horizon
Cesar Chavez's Birthday
☾→♋ Moon enters Cancer 6:44 am

Wednesday 1
☾♋

April Fool's Day
◑ 5:21 am

Thursday 2
☾♋

☾☌♄ 2:48 pm
☾→♌ Moon enters Leo 1:27 pm

Friday 3
☾♌

Saturday 4

Maya Angelou's Birthday
☾→♍ Moon enters Virgo 4:19 pm

Sunday 5
☾♍

Four of Wands

Who are the Witches?

inveniam viam[6]

For thousands of years, the label of "Witch" has been slapped on people in society as a pejorative and inflammatory term. These "Witches" were people who were seen as too clever, too cunning, intimidatingly strong, a bit different, or too independent. The label was especially used as a weapon against women who did not fit society's standards of beauty, youth, and subservience. Far more than bullying and name calling (although such things often lead to far worse), the label of "Witch" carried a death sentence along with the confiscation of property. This was a very tragic situation if you were unlucky enough to own property coveted by neighbors or if you made another person's spouse jealous, or if you were just a little different than those around you. Witches were also an uncomfortable reminder of the old religions to the rising church's economic and religiopolitical structure of the Middle Ages.

Modern Witches have embraced the term Witch, not as a pejorative, but as a declaration of empowerment and freedom from opression. Those attributes that were feared by the masses and suppressed by the economic-religiopolitical structure of the Middle Ages are honored and respected by Witches; independence, strength, cunning, wisdom, thinking "outside the box", and living in harmony with the Earth.

Witches today are no strangers to discrimination based on gender, religion, age, appearance, etc. This is a primary reason that Witches accept such diversity into their "ranks". As of 2014, well over a million people in the United States identify as Pagan or Wiccan[7], and many more accept the term "Witch" as a label of power and respect.

Hundreds of people were surveyed for this year's almanac, and the overwhelming majority are solitary practitioners.[8] Let's look at some of those survey results to see how individuals walk their paths to illustrate the rich diversity and acceptance now present among Witches. Although no two practitioners have the same viewpoints, we found that

Monday 6

Tartan Day
☾→♎ Moon enters Libra 4:17 pm

Tuesday 7
☾♎

United Nations World Health Day
○ "Supermoon" 9:35 pm

🌍 Moon's closest approach this year

Wednesday 8

International Romani Day
☾→♏ Moon enters Scorpio 3:17 pm

Thursday 9
☾♏

National Library Worker's Day

Friday 10

☾→♐ Moon enters Sagittarius 3:36 pm

Saturday 11
☾♐

Sunday 12

Four of Cups

☆ Virginid Meteor Shower, midnight, SE horizon
International Day of Human Space Flight
Christian: Easter Sunday
☾→♑ Moon enters Capricorn 7:06 pm

they share the empowering attributes of the modern Witch. **You may not agree with anyone else's path, but you can learn a lot about yourself just by thinking about what speaks to you, and what doesn't.** When filling out surveys, people were invited to check a small collection of boxes with "labels" they felt fit them best. Although the selection was limited to just over a dozen, these are listed under each person's path summary.[*]

Kyler's Path

Witchcraft is a path of empowerment for me. It allows me to manifest the changes I want to see in "my" world in order to affect "the" world. I recognize the Earth as sacred and a big part of my practice comes from honoring it, celebrating the Sabbats and Esbats, discovering my own power and helping others in doing the same. I was bullied for 13 years at school, my family doesn't support who I am and several "friends" turned their back on me or wanted to force me into something I wouldn't do. Witchcraft gives me freedom, it gives me *choice* and gives me back my voice. For me, Witchcraft is my form of rebellion. From Venezuela | Accepts the labels: Pagan Witch, Solitary Witch, Eclectic Witch, LGBTQ+

Willow's Path

I consider myself an agnostic, Pagan Witch. I don't know that I believe in any God/Gods/Goddesses. They are all symbolic to me. Even the Christian god. I consider myself a grey Witch because if I feel something needs to be done I do it without regard to the threefold theory. I do both light and dark magick. I'm not in a coven because I love being able to practice as I please without worrying that someone won't accept my ways. Willow is from the U.S.A | Accepts the labels: Pagan Witch, Solitary Witch, Eclectic Witch, Other, Grey Witch

---

[*]   Those of you who take any of the author's classes know that the motto is "Try to save your labels for your herb cabinet." Still, we were curious to see the diversity of labels that individuals embrace.

Monday 13
☽♑

Scrabble Day

Tuesday 14
☽♑

Moon & Jupiter conjunction before
dawn near the SE horizon

◑ 5:56 pm

Wednesday 15

U.S. Federal Tax Day
Conjunction of the Moon and Saturn & Mars
View before dawn on the SE horizon
☽→♒ Moon enters Aquarius 2:38 am

Thursday 16
☽♒

Mushroom Day
Margo Adler's Birthday

Friday 17

☽→♓ Moon enters Pisces 1:30 pm

Saturday 18
☽♓

Sunday 19
☽♓

Four of Pentacles

☀→♉ Sun enters Taurus 9:46 am
Bicycle Day: Albert Hoffman takes his historical bicycle trip 1943

January
10th -1:21pm

December
29th -9:28pm

February
9th -1:33am

November
30th -3:29am
Eclipse

2020

March
9th -12:47pm
Super

October
31st -9:49am
Blue

The Thirteen Full Moons

April
7th -9:35pm
Super

October
1st -4:05pm

Witches celebrate Esbats on the thirteen Full
Moons of the year. Some traditions (and devotees of
certain Goddesses) hold Esbats on the New Moon.
See the Dark Moons & New Moons area for a list
of New Moon dates and signs for 2020.

May
7th -5:45am

♓
September
2nd -12:22am

♒
August
3rd -10:58am

♑
July
4th -11:44pm
Eclipse

♐
June
5th -2:12pm

Distance of the Moon

Perigee: Pronounced *PER-uh-jee* Moon is closest to the Earth

Apogee: Pronounced *AP-uh-jee* Moon is farthest from the Earth

Perigee		Apogee		Perigee		Apogee	
Jan 13	2:20 pm	Jan 1	7:30 pm	Jul 25	12:01 am	Jul 12	2:26 pm
Feb 10	2:27 pm	Jan 29	3:26 pm	Aug 21	5:55 am	Aug 9	8:50 am
Mar 10	1:30 am	Feb 26	5:34 am	Sep 18	8:48 am	Sep 6	1:29 am
Apr 7	_1:08 pm_	_Mar 24_	_10:23 am_	Oct 16	6:46 am	Oct 3	12:22 pm
May 5	10:03 pm	Apr 20	2:00 pm	Nov 14	5:42 am	Oct 30	1:45 pm
Jun 2	10:38 pm	May 18	2:44 am	Dec 12	2:41 pm	Nov 26	6:28 pm
Jun 29	9:12 pm	Jun 14	7:56 pm			Dec 24	10:31 am

Underlined dates are the closest and farthest for the entire year.

Get your hands in the dirt

Monday 20

♁ Moon enters Aries 2:01 am

Tuesday 21

♈

Wednesday 22

🌍 Earth Day

● 9:25 pm

☽→♉ Moon enters Taurus 2:36 pm

Thursday 23

♉

☆ Lyrid Meteor Shower,
look NE at midnight
Order of the Garter Established

Friday 24

♉

Saturday 25

☽→♊ Moon enters Gemini 2:20 am

Sunday 26

♊

Five of Swords

Conjunction of Moon & Venus
western horizon at dusk

My Path

*	☽ 1 ✾		
Waxing	☽ 2		
	☽ 3		
	☽ 4 ✾		
	☽ 5		
Full	☽ 6		
	☽ 7		
	☽ 8		
	☽ 9		
	☽ 10		
	☽ 11		
	☽ 12		
	☽ 13		
Waning	☽ 14		
	(15 🚲		
	(16		
	(17		
	(18		
	(19		
	(20		
New	21		
	22		
	23		
	24		
	) 25		
	) 26		
Waxing	) 27		
	) 28		
	☽ 29		
	☽ 30		
	☽ 31		

May

Week	Mo	Tu	We	Th	Fr	Sa	Su
18					1	2	3
19	4	5	6	7	8	9	10
20	11	12	13	14	15	16	17
21	18	19	20	21	22	23	24
22	25	26	27	28	29	30	31

7:○   14:◐   22:●   29:◑

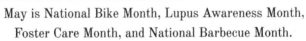

May is National Bike Month, Lupus Awareness Month,
Foster Care Month, and National Barbecue Month.

® Walking Your Path ◈

Herbalism Study: Chamomile, Clover, Lemon Balm
Stones to Study: Mahogany Obsidian,
                    Lapis Lazuli, Moonstone
Consider before Casting: Are you reacting to
something, or reflecting on it to find the best solution?

*The Sacred Lotus (Nelumbo nucifera), also known as Padma,
can produce heat in its flowers up to 86–95 °F (30–35 °C).*

[54]

Monday 27

☽→♋ Moon enters Cancer 12:28 pm

Tuesday 28
☽♋

Wednesday 29

☽☌♄ 11:26 pm
☽→♌ Moon enters Leo 8:06 pm

Thursday 30
☽♌

International Jazz Day
◐ 3:38 pm

Friday 1
☽♌

PaganPath.com founded, 1996

Saturday 2

☽→♍ Moon enters Virgo 12:36 am

Five of Wands

Sunday 3
☽♍

World Press Freedom Day

[55]

Beth's Path

I have strong faith in God (no need for gender) and Christ, and the Mother Mary. I'm not Catholic, I'm Protestant. But 'Granny Magic' or HooDoo has been a part of my life through my mother's side. Every woman for five generations has practiced HooDoo. It's about protection, healing, and turning negative energy away and back to the sender. There is no hate or revenge, it's about helping others learn not to do evil, bringing love, strength, and protection to those we love (or those we meet who ask). It is absolutely possible to believe in God, Christ, and have faith while using your manifesting energy for good. Granny Magic isn't going anywhere, it's has been around for centuries. I'm blessed to have it and the knowledge and that my daughter is finding her path in the same. | From the U.S.A.|Accepts label: Christian Witch

Skyler's Path

The divine or spirit is energy, not male or female, This energy moves through all things and is within each of us. It can be manifest into matter, and how we work with this energy defines us. I believe all paths are valid and try not to judge others. | From New Mexico, U.S.A. | Accepts the labels: Non-Religious Witch, Solitary Witch

Morgan's Path

I've been a Pagan for over forty years but didn't label my path until I found the term "eclectic". I do not like to follow anyone else's ways, so I study and use things that I'm drawn to no matter what path they come from. | From Wisconsin, U.S.A. | Accepts the labels: Pagan Witch, Eclectic Witch

A white rose symbolizes innocence, purity, and spirituality. *Many tarot decks depict the Fool card holding a white rose.*

Monday 4

7:49 pm

May the 4th be with you
☾→♎ Moon enters Libra 2:10 am

Tuesday 5
☾♎

Cinco de Mayo

Wednesday 6

η–Aquarid meteor shower
☾→♏ Moon enters Scorpio 2:05 am

Thursday 7
☾♏

○ 5:45 am

Friday 8

☾→♐ Moon enters Sagittarius 2:16 am

Saturday 9
☾♐

World Migratory Bird Day

Sunday 10

Five of Cups

Christopher Penezak's Birthday

Mother's Day

☾→♑ Moon enters Capricorn 4:39 am

Sunrise, Sunset & Twilight

The Sun's light has been charted here at intervals of about a fortnight. The hours of daylight do not change drastically from day-to-day, so every other week on the Sun's day (Sunday) you can check this chart to find the times of sunrise, sunset, and civil twilight. Civil twilight is a "tween" that is a very magical time* and is close to the same as the Golden Hour used in photography.

Working with the energy of tweens is very effective and quite easy. When civil twilight begins just before sunrise you can work toward new beginnings, fresh starts, financial growth, planting, etc. Civil twilight then ends at sunrise.

On the other end of the day, the sun sets and civil twilight begins, lasting just long enough to do a quick spell or magical working. The evening twilight is a bit more psychic and intuitive, and you can use its crackling energy for nearly any type of working.

Sunrise/set times may vary slightly in your area due to obstacles on your eastern or western horizon (such as a mountain or buildings), and due to your exact latitude. In addition, you can actually see the sun before it has crossed the horizon due to the refraction of Earth's atmosphere. This has already been accounted for in the data in your chart.

We often refer to the Equinoxes as times when day and night are equal in length. This isn't actually correct, and interestingly it is refraction that accounts for daylight being just a bit longer on the two Equinoxes. The actual term for equal day and night is Equilux, which usually occurs a few days before the Equinoxes.

Date (2020)	Twilight AM	Sunrise AM	Sunset PM	Twilight PM
Jan. 5	6:49	7:17	5:12	5:39
Jan. 19	6:47	7:14	5:24	5:52
Feb. 2	6:40	7:07	5:39	6:05
Feb. 16	6:28	6:54	5:52	6:18
Mar. 1	6:12	6:37	6:05	6:30
Mar. 15	6:53	7:18	7:17	7:42
Mar. 29	6:34	6:59	7:28	7:53
Apr. 12	6:14	6:40	7:39	8:05
Apr. 26	5:56	6:23	7:50	8:17
May 10	5:42	6:09	8:01	8:29
May 24	5:31	6:00	8:12	8:41
Jun. 7	5:26	5:55	8:20	8:50
Jun. 21	5:26	5:56	8:25	8:55
Jul. 5	5:32	6:01	8:25	8:55
Jul. 19	5:41	6:10	8:20	8:48
Aug. 2	5:52	6:20	8:09	8:37
Aug. 16	6:04	6:30	7:55	8:21
Aug. 30	6:15	6:41	7:37	8:03
Sep. 13	6:25	6:51	7:17	7:43
Sep. 27	6:36	7:01	6:57	7:23
Oct. 11	6:46	7:12	6:38	7:04
Oct. 25	6:58	7:23	6:21	6:47
Nov. 8	6:10	6:36	5:08	5:35
Nov. 22	6:23	6:50	5:00	5:27
Dec. 6	6:35	7:02	4:57	5:25
Dec. 20	6:44	7:12	5:01	5:29

Daylight Savings Time (noted on left side of chart, Mar. 15 – Nov. 8)

* For more information on tweens, Golden Hour and twilight, see the 2019 Practical Witch's Almanac.
  Lux is Latin for light, Nox is Latin for night. Daylight Savings Time accounted for in chart.

Monday 11
☾♑

Tuesday 12
Conjunction of the Moon with Jupiter & Saturn
  view before dawn near the SE horizon
International Nurses Day
☾→♒ Moon enters Aquarius 10:39 am

Wednesday 13
☾♒

α–Scorpiid Meteor Shower

Thursday 14
◗ 9:02 am
☾→♓ Moon enters Pisces 8:25 pm
Moon & Mars conjunction, pre-dawn SE horizon

Friday 15
☾♓

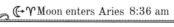

National Bike to Work Day

Saturday 16
☾♓

Sunday 17
Five of Pentacles

☾→♈ Moon enters Aries 8:36 am

The Pendulum

The pendulum is a wonderful method of divination falling under the category of **dowsing** (not scrying[9] as it is often referred to since being featured on the television series *Charmed*.) Dowsing is an ancient practice still in use by people all over the world, and a wide variety of methods are employed in its practice. *Water witching* is a form of dowsing that uses a Y shaped branch or two bent metal rods to discover water, metals or other materials under the ground. Its success has ensured that the practice has endured to the present, and many well diggers have a *dowser* they call upon before drilling new wells.

A pendulum is a simple cord with a weight on the end (the *bob*). You can purchase pendulums or make your own. It is easiest to use an item with a bit of heft for the bob. A string or cord with a swivel ensures that the bob does not have a tendency to simply swing up and down or side to side. A military-style beaded chain can be used in place of a swivel. Incorporating crystals, stones, herbs, and other materials into the bob is practical, and amethyst or quartz are popular.

The pendulum has maintained its place in our evolving world. An old tradition from the matriarchs on my Czech, German, and Irish lineage was to use a pendulum when the gender of an unborn child seemed somehow important. A wedding ring from someone on the maternal side of the family was strung onto a strand of hair from the pregnant woman. This makeshift pendulum is then held above the womb. Deosil or up-and-down movements meant male and widdershins or side-to-side movements meant female.[10]

A pendulum board is used to help answer complex questions, but simple yes and no questions do not need a board. The pendulum will indicate *yes* with up and down or deosil swings, and *no* being side to side or widdershins movements. **Yes/No questions are the easiest way to get started with pendulum practice**, and a pendulum board can be found on page 66 for questions that require more detailed answers.

Monday 18

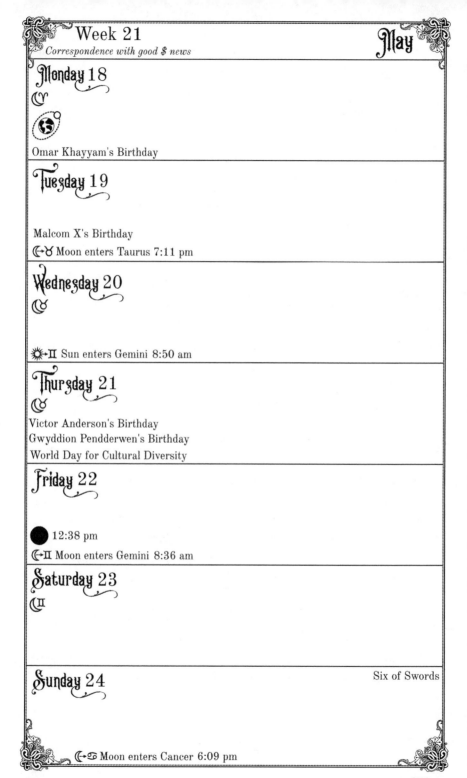

Omar Khayyam's Birthday

Tuesday 19

Malcom X's Birthday
☾→♉ Moon enters Taurus 7:11 pm

Wednesday 20
☾♉

☀→♊ Sun enters Gemini 8:50 am

Thursday 21
☾♉

Victor Anderson's Birthday
Gwyddion Pendderwen's Birthday
World Day for Cultural Diversity

Friday 22

● 12:38 pm
☾→♊ Moon enters Gemini 8:36 am

Saturday 23
☾♊

Sunday 24

Six of Swords

☾→♋ Moon enters Cancer 6:09 pm

Questions requiring more complex answers can present a challenge when you try to create a board that is evenly divided into sections. The multi-purpose board provided (page 66) can be used as-is or as a template. If you wish to make your own board, you can cover the one provided with thin paper and trace any of the divisions you prefer.

~ The outermost arc is 26 divisions, perfect for the alphabet.

~ The second arc has 24 divisions, great for the Elder Futhark runes.

~ The third arc is divided into 22, great for the tarot (and you will notice this ring is numbered with the Major Arcana designations).

~ The fourth ring is divided into 12, perfect for the months.

~ The fifth ring is divided into 10, to help with dowsing for numbers.

~ The sixth ring is divided into 7, great for the Chakras (marked) and the major colors of the rainbow (also marked).

~ The inner ring is divided into 4, you can write in anything you like, such as the four elements, four choices you are deciding among, etc.

Using Your Pendulum

Set the tip of your pendulum bob on the small dot at the middle-bottom of the board. Focus on your question and gently lift, allowing it to gently swing. The pendulum will begin to swing along a division in your board indicating your answers. If this feels awkward at first, don't worry it gets much easier with practice. Pendulums are useful and portable tools for developing your intuitive skills. You may find that with a pendulum, you have no need for other divinatory tools. Many pendulums can be worn as a necklace or pendant, so you always have one on hand. Now that's practical!

Week 22
Travel and rest, psychically and spiritually

Monday 25
☾♋

U.S. Federal Holiday: Memorial Day

Tuesday 26
☾♋

Wednesday 27

☽☌♄ 4:42 am
☾→♌ Moon enters Leo 1:33 am
Morning Glory Zell-Ravenheart's Birthday

Thursday 28
☾♌

Friday 29

◑ 10:29 pm
☾→♍ Moon enters Virgo 6:40 am

Saturday 30
☾♍

Joan of Arc Day

Sunday 31

Six of Wands

☾→♎ Moon enters Libra 9:38 am

My Path

○ 1	Waxing *		
○ 2			
○ 3			
○ 4			
○ 5	Full		
○ 6			
○ 7			
● 8			
● 9			
● 10			
● 11			
● 12	Waning		
● 13			
(14			
(15			
(16			
' 17			
18			
19			
20 ✸	New		
21			
22			
23			
) 24			
) 25	Waxing		
) 26			
) 27			
● 28			
● 29			
○ 30			

June

Week	Mo	Tu	We	Th	Fr	Sa	Su
23	1	2	3	4	5	6	7
24	8	9	10	11	12	13	14
25	15	16	17	18	19	**20**	21
26	22	23	24	25	26	27	28
27	29	30					

5 ○   13 ◑   21 ●   28 ◐

June is LGBT Pride Month, National Oceans Month,
National Adopt a Cat Month, and Candy Month

☾ Walking Your Path ♈

Herbalism Study: St. John's Wort, Mullein, Basil

Stones to Study: Kyanite, Watermelon Tourmaline, Hematite

Consider before Casting: How will my a spell make me feel? ☐ regretful ☐ grateful ☐ ashamed ☐ vindicated ☐ happy ☐ justified ☐ powerful ☐ balanced ☐ whole ☐ loved ☐ wise ☐ embarrased

For most baking, the liquid from canned chickpeas can be used as a vegan egg replacer. Use 2 tablespoons liquid to equal 1 egg.

Monday 1
☾♎

Tuesday 2
☾→♏ Moon enters Scorpio 11:06 am

Wednesday 3
☾♏

Marion Zimmer Bradley's Birthday

Thursday 4

☾→♐ Moon enters Sagittarius 12:17 pm

Friday 5
☾♐

Penumbral Lunar Eclipse
World Environment Day
○ 2:12 pm

Saturday 6

☾→♑ Moon enters Capricorn 2:45 pm

Sunday 7
☾♑

Six of Cups

British Museum Founded 1753

Monday 8

World Oceans Day

Moon conjuction Saturn & Jupiter
SE horizon, pre-dawn

☾→♒ Moon enters Aquarius 7:54 pm

Tuesday 9
☾♒

Wednesday 10
☾♒

☆☆ Ophiuchid Meteor Shower

Thursday 11

☾→♓ Moon enters Pisces 4:32 am

Friday 12
☾♓

Anne Frank's Birthday

Moon & Mars conjuction, view on SE horizon pre-dawn

Saturday 13

Gerald Gardner's Birthday

🌓 1:23 am

☾→♈ Moon enters Aries 4:03 pm

Sunday 14

Six of Pentacles

☾♈

World Blood Donor Day

Bailey's Path

I don't separate Deity into sexual polarities and do not adhere to organizational forms such as patriarchy and matriarchy, but rather believe that gender should not matter. I belong to a small coven in which decisions and ritual workings are based on the unity of a circle. Each covener takes turns coming up with ideas for ritual and there is no High Priest or High Priestess. Leadership cycles among coveners. From Colorado, U.S.A. | Accepts the label: Witch, Other

Emily's Path

My Goddess is Gaea, the primal mother of all things. My views are animistic-like, in that the Goddess is present everywhere, and that Mother Earth is a living entity with consciousness. I believe that the God is the Sun which brings light and life to the creative womb of the Earth. | From Canada | Accepts the label: Witch

Robin's Path

It was many years before I finally embraced my inner Witch and Pagan beliefs. Since that time, I have been trained and initiated in the Celtic Taibhsear and New Reformed Orthodox Order of the Golden Dawn (NROOGD) traditions by tradition founders. Since 2002, I have been a member of the international Sisterhood of Avalon and have found the Avalonian Tradition to feel most like home. Living in Washington state (U.S.A.), I have ample opportunity to connect with the elements through the forests, oceans, rivers, and mountains. Service to *source* is important to me, and I express this through taking care of the land I live on, serving on the board of the SOA, writing for publications and teaching workshops locally and nationally. |Accepts the Labels: Pagan Witch, Solitary Witch, Other

Shredded, post-circulation currency is a great addition to money spells.

Monday 15
♈

Tuesday 16

☾→♉ Moon enters Taurus 4:36 am

Wednesday 17
☾

Starhawk's Birthday
☿℞ Mercury Retrograde 11:59 pm

Thursday 18

☾→♊ Moon enters Gemini 9:00 pm

Friday 19
☾♊

Juneteenth

Saturday 20
☾♊

✦ Ophiuchid Meteor Shower
World Refugee Day
☀→♋ Sun enters Cancer 4:44 pm

4:44 pm

Sunday 21
Seven of Swords

Annular Solar Eclipse
International Day of Yoga

● 1:41 am   Father's Day
☾→♋ Moon enters Cancer 1:02 am

A Witchy Crossword

Across

1. The point when we are close to the Sun
2. Thujone rich herb in absinthe
3. Energy field around person or object
4. Sylphes are spirits of the element ____.
5. A drink poured out as an offering
6. Advice or counsel, the Wiccan ____
7. Shadow (Latin)
8. Almost, or nearly shadow (Latin)

Down

1. Nightshade family root said to scream
2. Sun crosses the celestial equator at ____
3. Latin for hidden or secret (think Tarot)
4. A besom is a Witch's ____
5. A gnome is an elemental spirit of ____
6. Elder wise woman (triple Goddess phase)
7. An animal (or other critter) closely bonded to a Witch or practitioner
8. Divination with cards
9. Healing succulent houseplant
10. Tarot's Major and Minor
11. Light of a celestial object obscured
12. Moon is farthest away at ____
13. Closest approach of the Moon
14. Lunar celebration

* Answer key at back of Almanac *

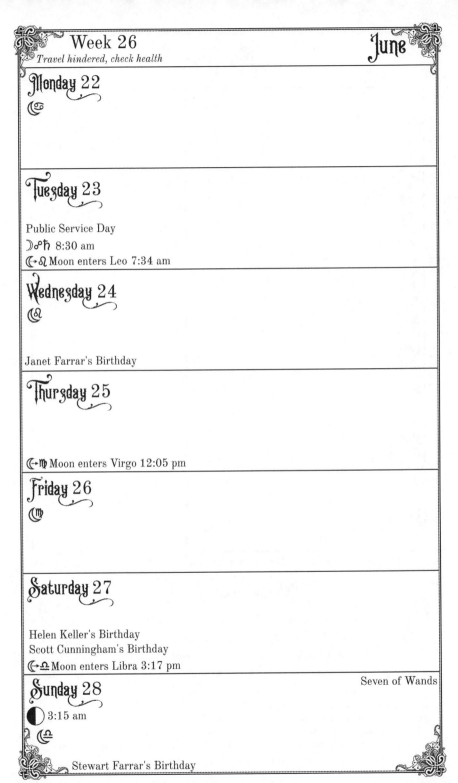

Monday 22

☽ ♋

Tuesday 23

Public Service Day
☽ ☍ ♄ 8:30 am
☾→♌ Moon enters Leo 7:34 am

Wednesday 24

☾ ♌

Janet Farrar's Birthday

Thursday 25

☾→♍ Moon enters Virgo 12:05 pm

Friday 26

☾ ♍

Saturday 27

Helen Keller's Birthday
Scott Cunningham's Birthday
☾→♎ Moon enters Libra 3:17 pm

Seven of Wands

Sunday 28

◗ 3:15 am

☾ ♎

Stewart Farrar's Birthday

My Path

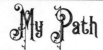

Week	Mo	Tu	We	Th	Fr	Sa	Su
27			1	2	3	4	5
28	6	7	8	9	10	11	12
29	13	14	15	16	17	18	19
30	20	21	22	23	24	25	26
31	27	28	29	30	31		

5 ○   12 ◑   20 ●   27 ◐

Full / Waxing
○ 1
○ 2
○ 3
◔ 4
◔ 5
◔ 6
◑ 7
◑ 8
◑ 9
◑ 10
◑ 11

Waning
◖ 12
◖ 13
◖ 14
◖ 15
◖ 16
◖ 17
◖ 18

New
19
20
21
22
23

Waxing
)24
)25
)26
)27
◗ 28
◗ 29
◗ 30
◗ 31

July is National Ice Cream Month and National Cell Phone Courtesy Month.

☩ Walking Your Path ☽

The Hanged Man

Herbalism Study: Yarrow, Calendula, Rowan
Stones to Study: Green Aventurine, Citrine, Garnet
Consider before Casting: How would my 10 year self see me today? Can I be "looked up to"?

Death

For a few weeks in of the year, the star Sirius (the Dog Star) rises just before the Sun on the eastern horizon. This is called "Heliacal Rising of Sirius" and marks the start of the ancient Egyptian calendar due to the star's association with the rebirth of the Nile. These "Dog Days" tend to be hot and humid in the northern hemisphere (NH), and calendars usually note them from July 3 to August 11. Actual dates vary by latitude, but for of NH, you'll be able to see Sirius in the days after August 10th.

Monday 29

☾→♏ Moon enters Scorpio 5:48 pm

Tuesday 30
☾♏

International Asteroid Day

Wednesday 1

☾→♐ Moon enters Sagittarius 8:21 pm

Thursday 2
☾♐

Thurgood Marshall's Birthday

Friday 3

U.S. Federal Holiday: Independence Day Observed
☾→♑ Moon enters Capricorn 11:48 pm

Saturday 4
☾♑

U.S. Independence Day
Penumbral Lunar Eclipse

○ 11:44 pm

Aphelion: Earth farthest from sun this year

Seven of Cups

Sunday 5
☾♑

Moon & Jupiter conjunction, SE horizon, pre-dawn

Kelly's Path

I started my studies in a Gardnerian coven, but after only a few months with them, I moved to a city very distant from my home coven. Now I'm with an Alexandrian coven which practices close to my views of Deity. I see the God as aspected in the Oak King of the Waxing year (Yule to Midsummer) and the Holly King of the Waning year (Midsummer to Yule). The God in both aspects dies and is reborn. The Goddess also changes in her aspects as Earth Mother and the lunar Queen of Heaven. | From Texas, U.S.A. | Accepts the labels: Alexandrian Witch

Linday's Path

I picked up a book by Marion Weinstein in the early '90s and never looked back. I worship the triple Moon Goddess (Diana, Selene, Hecate) and Sun God in two phases- Kernunnos (balance and inspiration) and Pan (flexibility and sensuality). My pentacle represents these five aspects of Deity. | From New York, U.S.A. | Accepts the labels: Dianic Wiccan, Solitary Witch

Jacobs Path

For me, Gods and Goddesses are separate entities, not simply facets of the All or One Deity. For thousands of years, people have worshiped very specific Deities, and through their worship, they have created energy pockets, a sort of collective memory or morphogenetic field (as Rupert Sheldrake describes them). I feel a close connection to certain Deities and have developed a relationship with some through meditation and shamanic practices. I use runes in my magical and divinatory practices and use certain runes to represent Odin and other patron Deities on my altar. | From Missouri, U.S.A. | Accepts the labels: Norse Pagan, Pagan Witch, Eclectic Witch

-84-

With Earth, Air, Water, and Fire, I enchant this charm to achieve my desire.

Monday 6

Conjunction Moon & Saturn
  SE horizon, pre-dawn
☽→♒ Moon enters Aquarius 5:09 am

Tuesday 7
☽♒

Wednesday 8

✦ Capricornid Meteor Shower
☽→♓ Moon enters Pisces 1:13 pm

Thursday 9
☽♓

Friday 10
☽♓

Saturday 11

World Population Day
☽→♈ Moon enters Aries 12:06 am

Seven of Pentacles

Sunday 12
☽♈

🌓 6:28 pm 🜨
☿ Mercury Direct 3:26 am

[75]

Protection Spell

This spell is designed to bless and protect you and your home and will create a permanent ward against baneful influence. Perform a cleansing both physically and psychically before you cast this spell.

Find a small bottle, flask, or box to hold the ingredients for this warding. Enter the meditative state in which you work magic, and collect a pinch of soil from the four corners of your property. If you live in an apartment, condo or high-rise, you can collect dust or fibers from the four corners inside your home.

Hold your container and visualize a barrier between your domain and the outside world (your threshold). Continue this visualization while pouring energy into your barrier and while adding three pinches of sea salt to the material in your container. While adding the salt, speak or chant any words of power that you prefer, or use:

Three times three my spell is bound

no bane shall cross this protected ground.

Once you feel that you have finished empowering your ward, seal it with *"So Mote it Be"* (So it Is or It is Done). You can bury it, place it on the mantle, put it under your bed, or tuck it into the back of a closet or drawer. Any place in the home it is protecting will do.

Repeat your visualization and empowerment of the ward every year or so, or whenever you feel it weakening. You can add items to the bottle or box to focus and energize the ward. Use the Directories to help you when selecting herbs, stones, crystals, runes, or other items.

You might also consider adding a strand of hair from each person or something from each animal that resides in your home.

Monday 13

Margaret Murray's Birthday
☽→♉ Moon enters Taurus 12:34 pm

Tuesday 14
☽♉

Jupiter opposite Sun

Wednesday 15
☽♉

☄ Capricornid Meteor Shower

Thursday 16

☽→♊ Moon enters Gemini 12:19 am

Friday 17
☽♊

Conjunction Moon & Venus, pre-dawn east horizon
📅 😂 🎂 🎉 🤫 😍 ❤️ 😊 World Emoji Day

Saturday 18

Nelson Mandela Day
☽→♋ Moon enters Cancer 9:24 am

Eight of Swords

Sunday 19
☽♋

Incense Recipes

Circle Incense

1 🔲 Myrrh

2 🔲 Benzoin

1 🔲 Ginger Root powder

6 🔲 Sandalwood chips or 3 🔲 powder

1 🔲 Cinnamon, ground

1 🔲 Frankincense

1 🔲 Copal

1 🔲 Cloves, whole crushed or ½ 🔲 ground

Circle incense can be used for any magical or spiritual purpose and is particularly well suited to blessing, purification, and adding energy to any spellwork. The recipe will create an incense much like "High Altar" used in many magical traditions, particularly in the south-east U.S. It developed as a lucky accident while creating Kyphi incense (a traditional Egyptian incense). As each ingredient was added, the fragrance of the blend was tested over incense charcoals. This formula was found to work better and have a better fragrance than most High Altar and Kyphi blends.

Yule Incense

6 🔲 Dried, crushed Pine Needles

1 🔲 Frankincense

1 🔲 Copal

1 🔲 Myrrh

2 🔲 Benzoin

Collect your ingredients for Yule incense now so you have everything in time for the Sabbat. This incense is delightful throughout the autumn and winter seasons.

Clarity incense developed after many years of burning bundles of sage to cleanse, purify, and bless. Although these bundles are great tools, they are not always practical for two important reasons. First, they put out more smoke that is usu-

Clarity Incense

6 🔲 Crushed White Sage

1 🔲 Frankincense

1 🔲 Copal

ally desirable indoors or for clearing people, crystals, or altar tools. Second, bundles drop a lot of ash and sparks, which is hard on fabrics and often dangerous. It is also a great incense for study and reading.

All recipes here are to be used on special incense charcoals.

Monday 20

Saturn at opposition

● 12:32 pm

) ☌ ♄ 12:54 pm

☾→♌ Moon enters Leo 3:16 pm

Tuesday 21

☾♌

☆ ☆ α–Cygnid Meteor Shower

Wednesday 22

☀→♌ Sun enters Leo 3:37 am

☾→♍ Moon enters Virgo 6:40 pm

Thursday 23

☾♍

Friday 24

☾→♎ Moon enters Libra 8:54 pm

Saturday 25

☾♎

Sunday 26

Eight of Wands

☾→♏ Moon enters Scorpio 11:12 pm

My Path

○ 1 ☉		
○ 2		
○ 3		
○ 4		
○ 5		
◐ 6 ☉		
◑ 7		
◑ 8		
◑ 9		
◑ 10		
◐ 11		
◖ 12		
◖ 13		
◖ 14		
◖ 15		
' 16		
17		

August

Week	Mo	Tu	We	Th	Fr	Sa	Su
31						**1**	2
32	3	4	5	**6**	7	8	9
33	10	11	12	13	14	15	16
34	17	18	19	20	21	22	23
35	24	25	26	27	28	29	30
36	31						

3 ○   11 ◐   18 ●   25 ◑

Full / Waning / New / Waxing (side labels)

18
19
20
21
22
23
24
25
26
27
28
29
30
31

August is National Picnic Month and Water Quality Month.

⟨ⓈⓌalking Ⓨour PathⓂ⟩

Herbalism Study: Verbena, Mugwort, Mint
Stones to Study: Celestite, Apache Tears, Amethyst
Consider before Casting: Will this spell work on a symptom, or does it go after the cause?

The triquetra or "trinity knot" is a Celtic symbol that represents a unity of three and is used as a symbol of protection and blessing. It has been used to signify the triple-Goddess for centuries, and to symbolize the Holy Trinity since the early Christian period. It is also used by some Celtic Reconstructionists to represent Lands, Sea, and Sky. ☘ Sometimes appears sans circle→⟁

Monday 27
☾♍

◑ 7:32 am

Tuesday 28
☾♍

Wednesday 29

✦ δ–Aquarid Meteor Shower
☾→♐ Moon enters Sagittarius 2:25 am

Thursday 30
☾♐

World Friendship Day

Friday 31

☾→♑ Moon enters Capricorn 6:59 am

Saturday 1
☾♑

Conjunction Moon & Jupiter, SE horizon after sunset

Sunday 2

Eight of Cups

✦ α–Capricornid Meteor Shower

Conjunction Moon & Saturn, SE after sunset
☾→♒ Moon enters Aquarius 1:11 pm

The Louche

An interesting thing can happen when you are trying to make Florida Water or perfume with essential oils and low-proof alcohol. Rum and Vodka are popular alcohol choices and are usually under 50% alcohol (25 proof or less). When you add more oils than can be kept in solution by the alcohol, some of the oils begin to cause your brew to become milky and opalescent. This is known as the *bloom*.

Although this bloom is desirable in an Absinthe beverage, you can correct this in your fragrances by slowly adding high-proof alcohol (95% alcohol / 180 proof) until your solution clarifies. If left uncorrected, a separate layer will eventually form as the precipitate oil molecules collect together (as seen in vinegar and oil salad dressing).

This is called the Louche (pronounced loosh, lewsh, or luʃ) and is also known as the French Method or the ouzo effect. This effect is harnessed in the creation of microencapsulated ingredients in cosmetics, and even nanoencapsulated materials for science and industry.

Theban Script

A	B	C	D	E	F	G
H	I	J	K	L	M	N
O	P	Q	R	S	T	U
V	W	X	Y	Z		

---

* The Theban Alphabet first appeared in the book entitled, *The Magus* in 1801. Modern Witches use it as a substitution cipher to encode spells from prying eyes, and to lend writing an air of mystery.

Monday 3
☾≈

○ 10:58 am

Tuesday 4

☾→♓ Moon enters Pisces 9:28 pm

Wednesday 5
☾♓

Thursday 6
☾♓

⊕ 8:04 pm

✦ τ–Aquarid meteor shower

Friday 7

☾→♈ Moon enters Aries 8:05 am

Saturday 8
☾♈

Sunday 9

Eight of Pentacles

🌑 National Book Lovers Day

Conjunction of Moon & Mars, before sunrise, east

☾→♉ Moon enters Taurus 8:28 pm

Ariel's Path

I can relate to many different views of deity but I don't hold a specific view of my own. I've had some visions during meditation of what seems to be a Goddess. I've also had some experiences where I was able to send up a shield to prevent a traffic collision that should have been fatal. I'm open to new ideas and am learning how to use my natural abilities, but I don't want to commit to a specific deity or religious path. | From Arizona, U.S.A. | Accepts the label: Non-Religious Witch

Michael's Path

I grew up Catholic and feel very close to Mary. My practice is eclectic, with Wicca incorporated into my relationship with Mary in the guise of the Goddess. I see Jesus as a symbol of the God. To the astonishment (and sometimes outrage) of many of my Wiccan friends, I have a statue of Mary and a cross on my altar. They still accept me anyway, and that is what I love about being a Witch. | From Iowa, U.S.A. | Accepts the labels: Christian Witch, Eclectic Witch

Cameron's Path

I grew up in New Orleans and combine Voudou with my Wiccan practices. I believe that the world was created by one God, who is both male and female. | From Louisiana, U.S.A. | Accepts the label: Witch

Carson's Path

I was trained in a traditional Gardnerian coven for a year and a day[11] but did not continue with initiation. My beliefs are eclectic and I believe that all deities are facets of the All, that all matter is energy and vice versa. | From London, England | Accepts the label: Witch

The circle is cast thrice about, to keep power in until it's let out.

Monday 10
☿

Tuesday 11
☿

🌗 11:44 am

Wednesday 12

☾→Ⅱ Moon enters Gemini 8:46 am

Thursday 13
☾Ⅱ

☄ Perseid Meteor Shower (NE sky around midnight, great shower!)

Friday 14

☾→♋ Moon enters Cancer 6:36 pm

Saturday 15
☾♋

Charles Godfrey Leland's Birthday
Conjunction Moon & Venus, east horizon before dawn

Sunday 16
Nine of Swords

☾♋

☽☍♄ 6:58 pm

Breakfast Biscotti

This recipe is a Sabbat and Esbat favorite for the cakes part of "cakes and ale". When you are too busy for breakfast, or simply have little interest in food in the morning, these biscotti will come in handy. The word biscotti means twice-cooked, and that is exactly what they are. Toasty, crunchy, and convenient, they will last for weeks in an airtight container.

Combine:

1/2 cup coconut oil (or oil of your choice)
6 drops anise or 8 drops star anise essential oil (optional)
1 cup coconut sugar (or regular granulated)
4 eggs

In a separate bowl combine:

2 1/4 cups whole wheat white flour or gluten-free all purpose flour
1 cup of your favorite protein powder, unflavored, chocolate, or vanilla
1 tablespoon baking powder
1/2 teaspoon sea salt

Combine the two bowls of ingredients to form a somewhat sticky dough. Add one or two of the Add-Ins* and shape into two low, flat loaves about 1 inch tall, 4 inches wide, and about 8-12 inches long. Bake at 350°F oven for 20-30 minutes or until firm and set, but not too browned. Remove from oven and allow the loaf to cool to almost room temperature.

Slice the loaf into 1/2 inch wide slices and return to the oven on racks to toast. Bake at 325°F for 10-15 minutes or until dry, crunchy, and toasty. Some protein powders brown at low temperatures, so if they are starting to get dark, reduce heat to 200°F and bake until dry and crunchy. Once cool, you can dip the bottoms or drizzle the tops with melted chocolate if you like.

---

* Optional Add-Ins: 1 cup shredded coconut, 1 cup toasted whole almonds, 1 cup pecans, 1 cup miniature chocolate chips, ¾ cup dried fruit (cranberries, acai, blueberries, elderberries)

Monday 17

☾→♌ Moon enters Leo 12:39 am

Tuesday 18

♌

● 9:41 pm

Wednesday 19

☾→♍ Moon enters Virgo 3:21 am

Thursday 20

♍

Friday 21

☆ α–Cygnid Meteor Shower
☾→♎ Moon enters Libra 4:16 am

Saturday 22

♎

☀→♍ Sun enters Virgo 10:45 am

Sunday 23

Nine of Wands

☾→♏ Moon enters Scorpio 5:16 am

Jessie's Path

My personal practice is eclectic, combining my beliefs with traditional Witchcraft and some traditional ideas that have been passed down through my family. I believe that there is truth within all spiritual paths and religions. I always respect the beliefs of others. I strive for balance and harmony with everything and everyone around me. For me, power comes from within and there is no <u>one</u> way to access that. Being a Witch keeps me grounded in the wisdom that no one else has the power to dictate my spirituality. I take what I have learned from my upbringing as a Christian and by combining it with my Witchcraft practices my love of God(ess) has evolved, deepened and enriched every aspect of my life. | From Georgia, U.S.A. |Accepts the Labels: Pagan Witch, Christian Witch, Solitary Witch, Eclectic Witch, Grey Witch, Alexandrian, Dianic, Norse Pagan

Luna's Path

I feel a close connection to the Goddess and the creative feminine energy of the Mother. I'm not comfortable with the idea of including a male "God" in my practice, particularly the Horned God, having come from a strict Christian background. I am devoted to the Goddess in her triple phase: Artemis/Diana the Maiden/New and Waxing Moon phase, Selene, the Mother/Full Moon phase, and Hecate, the Crone/Waning and Dark phase. I see the Goddess reflected in myths of the three fates, the cycles of the moon, and of life-death-rebirth. As a way to embrace my family's Irish heritage, I've begun studies of The Morrigan who has three phases, Ana (maiden or virgin) Babd (mother) and Macha (crone). My focus on the Goddess is a way to heal some of my past which involved abusive relationships and is a way to counterbalance our patriarchal society. | From North Dakota, U.S.A. | Accepts the labels: Dianic Wiccan, Solitary Witch, LGBTQ+

Monday 24

☾♏

Tuesday 25

◑

☾→♐ Moon enters Sagittarius 7:49 am

Wednesday 26

☾♐

Women's Equality Day

Thursday 27

☾→♑ Moon enters Capricorn 12:37 pm

Friday 28

☾♑

Moon & Jupiter conjunction, east after dusk

Saturday 29

☾→♒ Moon enters Aquarius 7:37 pm

Sunday 30   Nine of Cups

☾♒

Moon & Saturn Conjunction, east after dusk

My Path

	1	
Full	2	
	3	
	4	
	5	
	6	
	7	
Waning	8	
	9	
	10	
	11	
	12	
	13	
	14	
	15	
New	16	
	17	
	18	
	19	
	20	
	21	
	22 ✣	
	23	
Waxing	24	
	25	
	26	
	27	
	28	
	29	
	30	

September

Week	Mo	Tu	We	Th	Fr	Sa	Su
36		1	2	3	4	5	6
37	7	8	9	10	11	12	13
38	14	15	16	17	18	19	20
39	21	**22**	23	24	25	26	27
40	28	29	30				

2 ○   10 ◑   17 ●   23 ◐

September is Civic Awareness Month, National Wilderness Month,
National Courtesy Month, Chicken Month, Self Improvement Month,
Honey Month, and National Hispanic Heritage Month (Sept. 15-Oct.15)

ᚾ Walking Your Path ᛈ

Herbalism Study: Catnip, Ginger, Rue

Stones to Study: Amazonite, Bloodstone, Carnelian

Consider before Casting: What are my core ethical
values and how does my spellwork fit into them?

*September starts on the same day of the week as December each year but does
not end on the same day of the week as any other month in the year.*

Monday 31
☾♒

Raymond Buckland's Birthday

Tuesday 1

☾→♓ Moon enters Pisces 4:35 am

Wednesday 2
☾♓

○

Thursday 3

☾→♈ Moon enters Aries 3:22 pm

Friday 4
☾♈

World Sexual Health Day

Saturday 5
☾♈

Crazy Horse's Birthday
Moon & Mars Conjunction, east pre-dawn

Sunday 6

Nine of Pentacles

🌍

☾→♉ Moon enters Taurus 3:44 am

Celebrating the Sabbats

The eight Sabbats marked in your almanac are the most widespread and popular. However, any given Sabbat may have many names and your tradition may not incorporate all eight. Celebrating your Sabbats, particularly if you can go outdoors, will energize and recharge you. Over the years as you celebrate your Sabbats, you will instinctively feel them drawing near without even paying attention to the calendar.

Samhain is the beginning of the Wheel of the Year and is considered the "New Year" for many Witches. For some, this is the third and final harvest, and for many, it is a time to honor and celebrate ancestors. The "veil between the worlds" is thought to be thin and Witches use divination or call upon the spirits of those who have crossed over. Pronunciation of Samhain varies by tradition. Listed in order of most frequently used first: *SOW-en* (with the *ow* as in h<u>ow</u> or as in fl<u>ow</u>), *SOW-een*, and *SHAH-vin*.

Yule is also considered the New Year by some Witches and falls on the Winter Solstice. On Yule, we celebrate the rebirth of the Sun.

Imbolc brings an increase in warmth, the waxing of the light of the Sun and for many of us, the first stirrings of spring. This is a cross-quarter, falling about midway between the Solstice and Equinox.

Ostara is the Vernal or Spring Equinox. It is a time of rebirth within the Earth. Day and night are *approximately* equal.

Beltane is also a cross-quarter, being between the Equinox and the Solstice. As with Samhain, the "veil between the worlds" at Beltane is thought to be thin. The Earth is full of fertility, growth and abundance.

Midsummer is the Summer Solstice. This Sabbat is a celebration of the Sun at its peak and the warmth of the Earth. This is a very energetic time and traditionally a time for all types of spells and magic.

Lammas or Lughnasadh or Lughnassad is a time of harvest as the bounty of the earth is reaching maturity. For some, it is the first of three harvest Sabbats. Lughnassad is pronounced *LOO-nus-uh*.

Mabon is the Autumn Equinox and the second harvest for some. Celebrations of gratitude and the harvest are primary themes of this Sabbat.

Monday 7
☾♉

U.S. Federal Holiday: Labor Day

Tuesday 8

International Literacy Day
☾→♊ Moon enters Gemini 4:28 pm

Wednesday 9
☾♊

☆ Piscid Meteor Shower

Thursday 10
☾♊

◑ 4:25 am
Carl Llewellyn Weschcke's Birthday

Friday 11

Silver Ravenwolf's Birthday
☾→♋ Moon enters Cancer 3:23 am

Saturday 12
☾♋

International Programmers' Day

Sunday 13   Ten of Swords

☽☌♄ 2:36 am
☾→♌ Moon enters Leo 10:33 am

Conjunction of Moon & Venus, east before dawn

Decoding the Binomials

Listening to herbalists and botanists talk may seem like eavesdropping on a group of occultists speaking in strange ancient languages. There is no secret society here, just the spirit of academia. When we are exploring the world of plants, we must honor this spirit by embracing the nomenclature of the professionals. Once you start learning a few of the Latin and Greek roots of botanical binomials, you will be able to understand more about a plant just from its systematic name. This learning becomes addictive as the stories of plants and people unfold during your quest.

The words used in a botanical binomial may be a feminine or masculine version of the word. Not all variations are listed but you can easily extrapolate from this list. Below are a few definitions and a bit of etymology to get you started in your learning addiction.

agrestis: of or from the field, wild.

albus, alba, album: white. E.g. *Quercus alba* (White Oak) *Viscum album* (mistletoe, the name takes note of the white berries)

annuus: annual, occurs once a year

apis, apiana, apianus, apianum: bees, belonging to the bees, sought by or liked by the bees. *Salvia apiana* (Bee Sage)

aquaticus: found in or near water

arborescens: like a tree or shrub

borealis: northern

caulos: stem, stalk. Like cauliflower is a flowering stalk.

delphis: from the Greek δελφύς (delphús) meaning womb

digitalis, digitatus, digitata, digitatum: having fingers

dulcis: sweet

edulis: edible

folium: leaf, foliage. *Echinacea angustifolia* (Purple Coneflower)

glaucus, glauca, glaucum: blue-green, gray-blue, gleaming

graveolens: strong smelling. *Ruta graveolens* (Strong Smelling Rue, common Rue)

Monday 14
☾♌

Tuesday 15

☾→♍ Moon enters Virgo 1:38 pm

Wednesday 16
☾♍

World Ozone Layer Day

Thursday 17

● 6:00 am

☾→♎ Moon enters Libra 1:56 pm

Friday 18
☾♎

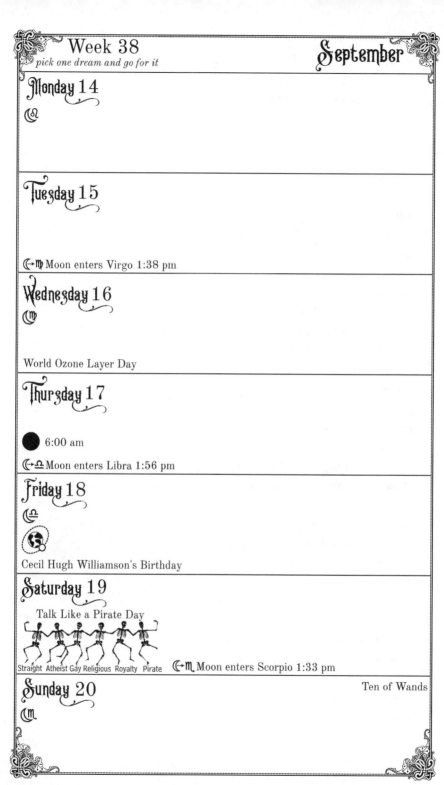

Cecil Hugh Williamson's Birthday

Saturday 19

Talk Like a Pirate Day

Straight Atheist Gay Religious Royalty Pirate   ☾→♏ Moon enters Scorpio 1:33 pm

Sunday 20
☾♏

Ten of Wands

helio: from the Greek from ἥλιος (hélios) meaning sun. *Helianthus annuus* (Annual Sunflower)

hirsutus, hirsuta, hirsutum: hairy. *Hypericum hirsutum* (Hairy St John's-wort)

indicus, indica, indicum: Indian. *Citrus indica* (Indian Wild Orange)

lact: milk. As in yogurt or keifir created by the bacterias *Lactobacillus bulgaricus*, *Lactobacillus acidophilus*, etc.

luteus, lutea, luteum: yellow color, saffron color

macro: large

maritima, maritimum, maritimus: Of the sea, marine. *Rosmarinum officinalis* (Rosemary).

micro: small

nucifera: nut bearing

occidentalis, occidentale: western

officinalis: of the shop, for the workshop[12], such as *Salvia officinalis* (Garden Sage) and *Rosa officinalis* (the Apothecary Rose)

orientalis, orientale: eastern

pallidus: pale

phyllo: From the Greek φύλλον (phúllon) for leaf

phyto: From the Greek φυτόν (phutón) for plant

purpureus: purple. *Echinacea purpurea* (Purple Cone Flower) *Digitalis purpurea* (Purple Foxglove - see **digitalis** to remember the glove part)

rhiza: root. *Xanthorhiza simplicissima* (Yellowroot) *Osmorhiza longistylis* s(Sweet Cicely, Aniseroot, Sweet Chervil)

ros: dew, moisture

ruber, rubra, rubrum, rubellus, rubrescens: red. *Acer rubrum* (Red Maple)

sapiens: wise

tinctorius, tinctoria, tinctorium: for dying. *Isatis tinctoria* (Woad)

Variegated leaves show different color zones, usually white or cream and green.

tomentosus, tomentosa, tomentosum: furry

variegatus, variegata, variegatum: variegated

vernus, vernalis, vernale: spring. e.g. Vernal Equinox

vulgaris, vulgare: common

xantho: yellow

Monday 21

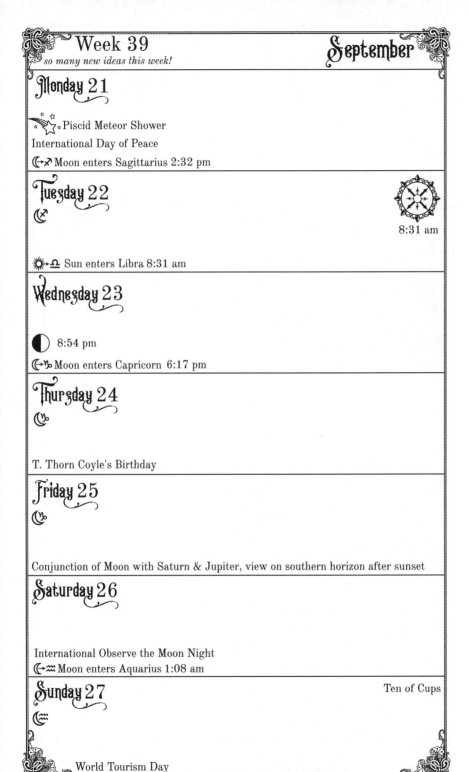 Piscid Meteor Shower

International Day of Peace

☾→♐ Moon enters Sagittarius 2:32 pm

Tuesday 22
☾♐

8:31 am

☀→♎ Sun enters Libra 8:31 am

Wednesday 23

◑ 8:54 pm

☾→♑ Moon enters Capricorn 6:17 pm

Thursday 24
☾♑

T. Thorn Coyle's Birthday

Friday 25
☾♑

Conjunction of Moon with Saturn & Jupiter, view on southern horizon after sunset

Saturday 26

International Observe the Moon Night

☾→♒ Moon enters Aquarius 1:08 am

Sunday 27
☾♒

Ten of Cups

World Tourism Day

My Path

Full ○ 1	
○ 2	
○ 3	
◔ 4	
◔ 5	
◑ 6	
◑ 7	
◑ 8	
◑ 9	
10	
(11	
(12	
13	
14	
15	

October

Week	Mo	Tu	We	Th	Fr	Sa	Su
40				1	2	3	4
41	5	6	7	8	9	10	11
42	12	13	14	15	16	17	18
43	19	20	21	22	23	24	25
44	26	27	28	29	30	**31**

1 ○ 9 ◑ 16 ● 23 ◐ 31 ○

New 16
17
18
)19
)20
)21
◑)22
◑)23
◑)24
◑)25
○)26
○)27
○)28
○)29
Full ○30
○31 ✿

October is Domestic Violence Awareness Month, Breast Cancer Awareness
Month, Diversity Awareness Month, and Black History Month (UK).

⬆ Walking Your Path ◇

Herbalism Study: Comfrey, Scullcap, Jasmine

Stones to Study: Amber, Jet, Botswana Agate

Consider before Casting: Are there any stones,
herbs, colors, or symbols that can lend their energies to my spell?

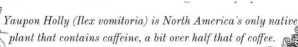

*Yaupon Holly (Ilex vomitoria) is North America's only native
plant that contains caffeine, a bit over half that of coffee.*

Monday 28

☾→♓ Moon enters Pisces 10:34 am

Tuesday 29
☾♓

World Heart Day

Wednesday 30

☾→♈ Moon enters Aries 9:48 pm

Thursday 1

○ 4:05 pm

Isaac Bonewits's Birthday
World Vegetarian Day

Friday 2
☾♈

Mahatma Gandhi's Birthday
Conjunction Moon & Mars, east pre-dawn

Saturday 3

☾→♉ Moon enters Taurus 10:13 am

Sunday 4   Ten of Pentacles
☾♉

Seeing Shadows?

Seeing shadows out of the corner of your eye is not that unusual. There are many reasons for this phenomenon from mundane to magical. Most paranormal investigators refer to this phenomenon as *shadow men* or *shadow people*, but occultists use the terms *shadow cats* and *witch cats*. There are many causes for seeing shadows, particularly in your peripheral vision. Let's begin with the mundane causes and then cover the possibilities from a practical Witch's perspective.

Chemical Causes

There are certain foods and chemicals that will increase the occurrence of witch cats. If you drink more coffee than usual, have less sleep than usual, change your sleep schedule frequently, or consume certain amphetamine and related compounds such as ADHD medication, you may see witch cats more frequently (and you may attract more attention from animals). Of course, if you are under the influence of a hallucinogen or have entered a shamanic mind state, it is to be expected that you will see a wide range of possible visual phenomena. This brings us to physical causes.

Physical & Physiological Causes

In addition to ingesting compounds or triggering chemicals in your mind, there are physiological causes for seeing shadows. Your eyes have both cones and rods. Peripheral vision is produced largely by retinal rod cells and these do not produce detailed resolution like the central cone cells. Rod cells sense light and movement, but not color like cone cells. This can cause low resolution, low color, fleeting movements to be perceived out of the corner of your eye (shadows).

The more attention that is given to this phenomenon, the more it will be observed due to visual substitutions.

Monday 5

World Teacher's Day
☾→Ⅱ Moon enters Gemini 11:03 pm

Tuesday 6
☾Ⅱ

Wednesday 7
☾Ⅱ

Arnold Crowther's Birthday

Thursday 8

☾→♋ Moon enters Cancer 10:46 am

Friday 9
☾♋

◑ 7:39 pm

Saturday 10

☽☌♄ 11:03 am
☾→♌ Moon enters Leo 7:25 pm

Sunday 11

Page of Swords

☾♌

When you have ambiguous, conflicting or insufficient sensory stimuli, your brain will resolve it by providing you with an interpretation. In other words, your brain will interpret the shadow image through its own expectation filter, providing you the image of a face, figure, cat, or other common human interpretation.

Paranormal Causes

As mentioned above, most paranormal investigators will quickly define the shadows you see as shadow men. Next, you may be informed that these shadow people are ghosts, demons, angels or lost spirits. These are all possible answers, but in my experience, they are not the most common. An exorcism is often recommended by paranormal and metaphysical workers.

A Practical Witchs Perspective

One of the most important skills a Witch can develop is to **observe without labeling**. There is no way we can know all the facts, so report what you see, not what you think you see. In other words, avoid filtering your observations through predefined expectations. Yes, you might be seeing time travelers or inter-dimensional beings, but there is no way to really know. Maybe they are ghosts, aliens or demons, who can truly say? What is important from a practical viewpoint is to observe and control how these shadows affect you and those around you.

That said, of course, I have my own solutions based on my observations. In my experiences, witch cats are a frequent infestation for Pagans and Witches who are dealing with a lot of stress or working a lot of magic. Some Witches do keep late hours (see the chemical and physiological causes above) but shadows do seem to appear more frequently to those who have strong psychic abilities. My current working theory is that extra energy from spellwork lingers and gathers in a sort of collection, like an energy dust bunny. They can become terrible,

Monday 12

☾→♍ Moon enters Virgo 11:56 pm

Tuesday 13
☾♍

Conjunction Moon & Venus, east pre-dawn
☿℞ Mercury Retrograde 8:05 pm

Wednesday 14
☾♍

Patricia Crowther's Birthday

Thursday 15

International Day of Rural Women
☾→♎ Moon enters Libra 12:54 am

Friday 16
☾♎

● 2:31 pm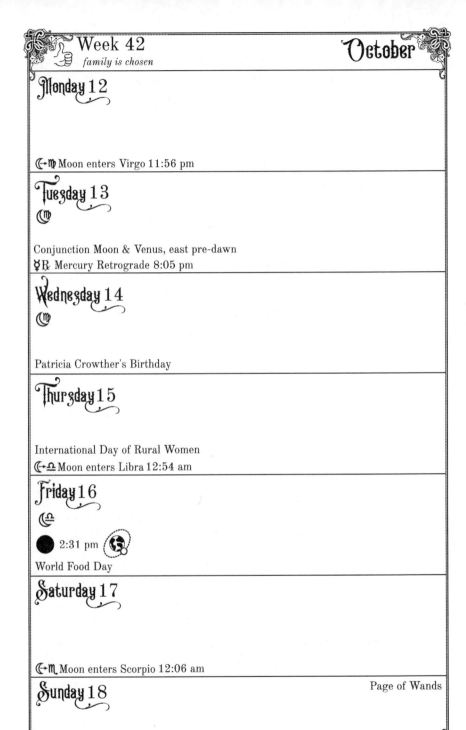

World Food Day

Saturday 17

☾→♏ Moon enters Scorpio 12:06 am

Sunday 18

Page of Wands

☾→♐ Moon enters Sagittarius 11:43 pm

even frightening (fear will feed them) but are actually very simple to remove. They can also be made more cohesive through negative attacks against you or your household. Similar to the classic "evil eye" these shadows appear more often when you are under magical attack, whether that attack is intentional or not.

- Once you have accumulated several observations, you can investigate to see if there are any common causes, mundane or magical, and turn these triggers off. The team at the almanac website has collected numerous reports and we have observed these shadows ourselves. Through this, we have found some common situations that cause the appearance of these shadows.

- The person observing the shadow is highly psychic, empathic, or has been performing a lot of magic.

- The person observing the shadow has been frequently meditating or entering shamanic states of consciousness.

- The area where shadows appear has a high energy charge.

- The area where shadows appear is often in "tweens" like doorways and windows, near the edges of magickal circles, near thresholds.

- The area where shadows appear has collected psychic and physical junk, such as stacks of paperwork, piles of clothes, un-cleansed crystals, boxes of things you were going to sort out someday, etc.

- An area has been cleared and cleansed, but no charge was provided in place of the cleared out energy. **This is a common problem.**

Often there is an accumulation of random energy and the more attention you give to the shadows the more cohesive and "manifest" they become. No matter what the cause for witch cats, shadow cats or shadow people (whatever you wish to call them) it is clear that the more energy, paranoia, or concern you provide them, the more frequently you will see them. From a magical perspective, you are feeding them energy, and from a psychological perspective, you are providing an anticipated identification for what you see.

the worst is behind you, and you phoenixed that!

Monday 19
☾♐

Tuesday 20
☾♐

Selena Fox's Birthday

Wednesday 21

☆ ☆
🌠☆ Orionid Meteor Shower
☾→♑ Moon enters Capricorn 1:44 am

Thursday 22
☾♑

☀→♏ Sun enters Scorpio 6:00 pm
Conjunction Moon with Saturn & Jupiter, view on southern horizon after dusk

Friday 23

◑ 8:22 am
☾→♒ Moon enters Aquarius 7:17 am

Saturday 24
☾♒

United Nations Day

Sunday 25

Page of Cups

☾→♓ Moon enters Pisces 4:19 pm

My Path

Full	○ 1 ⚙		
	○ 2		
	◐ 3		
Waning	◑ 4		
	◑ 5		
	◑ 6		
	◑ 7 ⚙		
	◖ 8		
	◖ 9		
	◖ 10		
	◖ 11		
	12		
	13		
New	14		
	15		
	16		
	17		
	◗ 18		
Waxing	● 19		
	◗ 20		
	◗ 21		
	◗ 22		
	◗ 23		
	◗ 24		
	○ 25		
	○ 26		
	○ 27		
	○ 28		
Full	○ 29		
	○ 30		

November

Week	Mo	Tu	We	Th	Fr	Sa	Su
44							1
45	2	3	4	5	6	7	8
46	9	10	11	12	13	14	15
47	16	17	18	19	20	21	22
48	23	24	25	26	27	28	29
49	30						

8 ◑   15 ●   21 ◐   30 ○

November is Native American Heritage Month, Epilepsy Month, Diabetes Awareness Month, National Adoption Awareness Month, and Caregivers Appreciation Month.

☌ Walking Your Path ☌

Herbalism Study: Sandalwood, Cinnamon, Cayenne

Stones to Study: Flourite, Clear Quartz, Goldstone

Consider before Casting: Imagine you go to the parking lot to find a bunch of teens you do not know inside your car. How would you react? What if you found out a few minutes later that you were mistaken, and that it is not your car?

If you enjoy puzzles like the crossword on page 70, check out PracticalWitch.com to download more this month. Some are easy and others will present a challenge.

Monday 26

Tuesday 27

DEL film shoot—
Dam breach

Wednesday 28

☾→♈ Moon enters Aries 3:45 am

Walk at night

Thursday 29

Conjunction of Moon & Mars, eastern horizon after dusk

Friday 30

☾→♉ Moon enters Taurus 4:19 pm

Saturday 31

Halloween
+ Blue Moon

○ 9:49 am "Blue Moon"

Sunday 1

Page of Pentacles

Day of the Dead
World Vegan Day

Samhain ~
Stay up all night!

⏰ U.S. Daylight Savings Time ends, clocks -1 hour at 2:00 am

Banishing Shadows

If you are infested with these shadows, it is best to do a thorough cleansing, but don't make the frequent mistake of cleaning everything out and leaving a vacuum.   After a cleansing ritual, the best protection is a new charge or blessing. Good options are for grounding, clarity, blessings, and peace.

Laughter, sunshine, fresh air, regular sleep, proper diet, standard physical cleaning, not giving the shadows too much power or attention, proper grounding and clearing of energy and charging cleared areas with a specific intent are all good housekeeping practices to keep them away for good. Just remember, relax, don't give them your fear, and don't feed the witch cats!

Monday 2

☾→♊ Moon enters Gemini 4:00 am

Tuesday 3
☾♊

Election Day

☿ Mercury Direct 11:50 am

Wednesday 4

☾→♋ Moon enters Cancer 3:46 pm

Thursday 5
☾♋

Use hottub!

☄ Taurid Meteor Shower

Friday 6
☾♋

Dad's bday

☾☌♄ 6:51 pm

Saturday 7

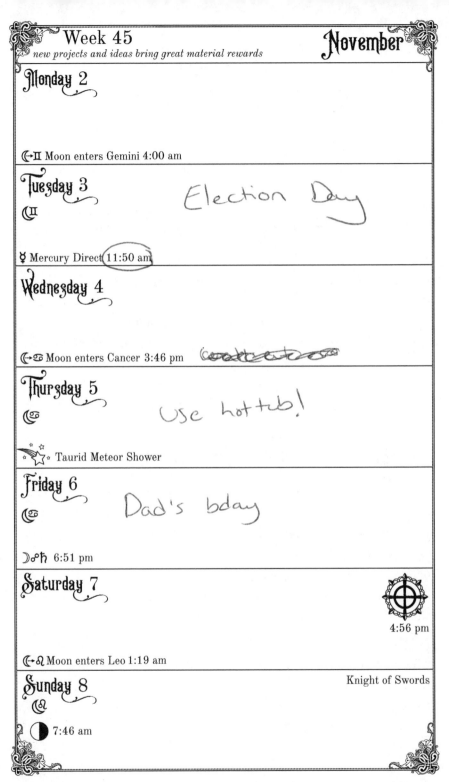

4:56 pm

☾→♌ Moon enters Leo 1:19 am

Sunday 8
☾♌

Knight of Swords

◐ 7:46 am

Étouffée

1 ½ lb of Shrimp, Crawfish, or Oyster Mushrooms (vegetarian)	1 can Cream of Mushroom Soup
1 medium Onion	1 can Cream of Celery soup
1 large Green Bell Pepper	1 can Diced Tomatoes w/Chilis
1 large Red Bell Pepper	2 tablespoons Butter or Oil
1 large Yellow Bell Pepper	Cajun seasoning (I prefer Louisiana Fish Fry brand étouffée seasoning. It is worth the extra effort to find it.)

This is an amazingly delicious, quick, and easy recipe. Even your friends from New Orleans will be shocked at how good this is. Chop the onion and peppers into a medium dice. Sauté onions in oil until they begin to carmelize. Add the peppers and sauté another minute. Add canned soups and tomatoes. Heat slowly, stir as needed to prevent scorching. When very hot ($170\,^\circ$F+) stir in the shrimp or mushrooms, season to taste, cover, wait another minute and then shut off the heat. Top with minced chives and serve over rice with crusty French bread.

Mountain Hash

This is another quick and easy recipe that is a staple for any mealtime in the hills of the Ouachita forest. Use leftover baked potatoes that have chilled overnight. For each person you are serving, use 2-3 eggs, 1 baked potato (leave the skin on for flavor/nutrients), ¼ chopped onion (or 1 tablespoon chives), and 2 ounces of any meat or mushrooms if you desire. Ham, bacon, sausage, brats, and polish ring all work well, or portabellas are a favorite. Top this with cheese if desired

Dice the potato into ½ inch cubes and fry in a hot cast iron skillet with a bit of oil until they begin to brown. Add the onions and sauté until softened and are beginning to take on a light caramelization. Add meat and/or mushrooms if desired and continue to stir-fry until cooked. Pour eggs over mixture, lower heat, stir gently until done.

Monday 9

☾→♍ Moon enters Virgo 7:30 am

Tuesday 10
☾♍

Wednesday 11

U.S. Federal Holiday: Veterans Day
☾→♎ Moon enters Libra 10:10 am

Thursday 12
☾♎

☄ Taurid Meteor Shower
Conjunction of the Moon & Venus, view pre-dawn on SE horizon

Friday 13

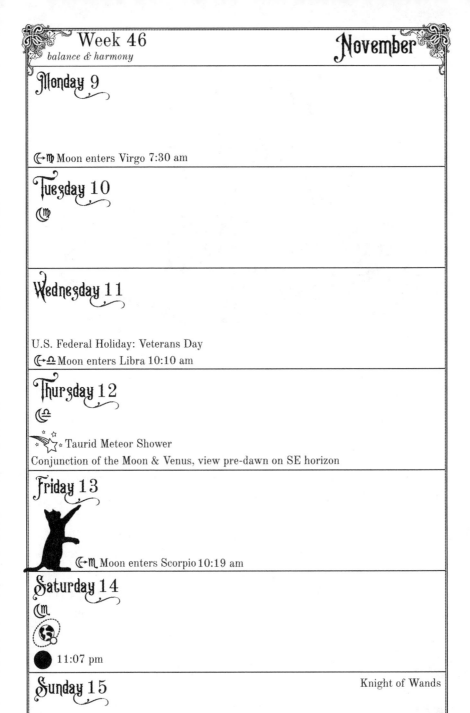

☾→♏ Moon enters Scorpio 10:19 am

Saturday 14
☾♏

● 11:07 pm

Sunday 15

Knight of Wands

☾→♐ Moon enters Sagittarius 9:47 am

Directories

These directories continue opposite of your planner pages for the weeks that follow. Use these directories as a launch pad for studying the prompts found in the Walking Your Path section at the beginning of each month.

The information in these Directories is similar to what you might find in an extensive Book of Shadows or magical correspondence. However, the botanical binomials of plants are up-to-date and keyword interpretations for divinatory arts are compiled from tens of thousands of actual readings. To make your research quick and easy, the emphasis in these Directories is on the practical, modern, and accurate.

Your monthly study prompts will send you to the first Directories within. Herbs for your wortcunning studies, Tarot and Runes for delving into the divinatory arts, and Stones, Crystals & Minerals for learning about these amazing gifts from the Earth. Additional Directories will help you round out your studies and can be used as a quick reference for your personal practice throughout the year. You might incorporate these Directories into your own Book of Shadows or magical journal, or save your Almanac for future reference.

Book drawing adapted by the author from a scan of a 1900 engraving in
Historic Byways and Highways of Old England by William Andrews

Monday 16
☾♐

International Day of Tolerance

Tuesday 17

Israel Regardie's Birthday
☾→♑ Moon enters Capricorn 10:35 am

Wednesday 18
☾♑

Hottub, !

☆ Leonid Meteor Shower

Thursday 19

World Philosophy Day
☾→♒ Moon enters Aquarius 2:25 pm

Conjunction of the Moon with Jupiter & Saturn, view on southern horizon pre-dawn

Friday 20
☾♒

Saturday 21
◗ 10:45 pm

Laura's bday

World Television Day
☀→♐ Sun enters Sagittarius 2:40 pm
☾→♓ Moon enters Pisces 10:06 pm

Sunday 22
☾♓

Knight of Cups

Herbs

This list of herbs contains some of the most useful magical and medicinal allies for stocking your wortcunning cupboard. Every attempt has been made to include the most popular herbs and plants to help with a multitude of situations.

Please note that many magical herbals contain outdated species names. This is because they all use the same small handful of reference materials. We are all fond of these old herbals, and extremely grateful for their existence. However, taxonomy changes and research continues. Modern Witches and herbalists embrace the most recent scientific research and that is reflected here with the <u>current</u> species names. No offense to our beloved "Ma Greeves"[*].

One look at the entries for sage and oregano will illustrate why it is so important to learn a plant's real name. This is not only critical in cooking and medicinal herbalism to prevent accidental poisoning, but it is also vital to magical herbalism and cultivation.[‡]

The "first name" of a plant listed is the genus, such as *Salvia*. The "second name" of a plant listed is the specific epithet, such as *officinalis*, and together they identify the species, *Salvia officinalis*. Sometimes a plant is the progeny of two species. To indicate that this is the case, a multiplication sign is used in the species name, e.g. *Lavender×intermedia*. To be taxonomically correct, a species name should be noted in italics, with the genus capitalized and the specific epithet lower-case. For the purposes of this list, species names have not been italicized.

Plants are listed in the order of appearance in your monthly study prompts in the My Path sections.

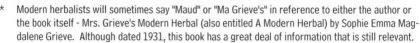

---

[*]   Modern herbalists will sometimes say "Maud" or "Ma Grieve's" in reference to either the author or the book itself - Mrs. Grieve's Modern Herbal (also entitled A Modern Herbal) by Sophie Emma Magdalene Grieve. Although dated 1931, this book has a great deal of information that is still relevant.

[‡]   Before ingesting any herb, consult a qualified health care practitioners to check for safety and possible interactions with any medications. *Natural* does not always mean *safe*.

Monday 23
☽♓

Tuesday 24

☽→♈ Moon enters Aries 9:05 am

Wednesday 25
☽♈

Conjunction of the Moon & Mars, view on eastern horizon after dusk

Thursday 26

U.S. Federal Holiday: Thanksgiving
☽→♉ Moon enters Taurus 9:43 pm

Friday 27
☽♉

"Black Friday"

Saturday 28
☽♉

Sunday 29

Knight of Pentacles

☽→♊ Moon enters Gemini 10:16 am

My Path

			December				
Week	Mo	Tu	We	Th	Fr	Sa	Su
49		1	2	3	4	5	6
50	7	8	9	10	11	12	13
51	14	15	16	17	18	19	**20**
52	21	22	23	24	25	26	27
53	28	29	30	31			

7 ☽   14 ●   21 ☽   29 ○

Full
○ 1
○ 2
○ 3
○ 4
○ 5
◑ 6
◑ 7

Waning
(8
(9
(10
(11
| 12

New
13
14
15
16

Waxing
17
18
19
20 ✷
21
◐ 22
◐ 23
◐ 24
◐ 25
○ 26
○ 27

Full
○ 28
○ 29
○ 30
○ 31

December is Bingo Month and Write to a Friend Month.

⊗ Walking Your Path ①

Herbalism Study: Frankincense, Myrrh, Bay

Stones to Study: Hawk's Eye, Ruby, Sapphire

Consider before Casting: Do I understand all the words used in this spell? If not, try to write your own.

"Jingle Bells" is a popular song at this time of year. It was composed in 1857 as a song for Thanksgiving rather than Christmas.

Monday 30
♊

"Cyber Monday"
◯ 3:29 am
Penumbral Lunar Eclipse

Tuesday 1

Eat a Red Apple Day
☾→♋ Moon enters Cancer 9:33 pm
First military grave marker with a pentacle allowed for veterans in 2007

Wednesday 2
☾♋

Thursday 3
☾♋

Friday 4

International Cookie Day
☽☌♄ 4:28 am
☾→♌ Moon enters Leo 6:53 am

Saturday 5
☾♌

Repeal Day
World Soil Day
International Volunteer Day

Sunday 6

Queen of Swords

 ☾→♍ Moon enters Virgo 1:47 pm

Rosemary - purification, memory, blessing
Rosmarinus officinalis
(roz-muh-RYE-nus uh-fiss-ih-NAY-lus)

Sage - purification, cleansing, blessing

- Salvia (SAL-vee-uh)
  S. officinalis - Common Garden Sage
  S. apiana - White Sage, Bee Sage, Sacred Sage
  S. sclarea - Clary Sage
- Artemisia (ar-te-MEE-see-uh)
  A. tridentata - Big Sagebrush, Basin Sagebrush
  A. californica - California Sagebrush

Rosemary

Garden
Sage

Wormwood - visions, astral projection, divination, love, lust

- Artemisia (ar-te-MEE-see-uh)
  A. absinthium - Wormwood
  A. dracunculus - French Tarragon

Lavender - love, protection, purification, peace, harmony, joy

- Lavandula (luh-VAN-dew-luh)
  L. angustifolia (formerly L. vera or L. officinalis) English lavender,
  French lavender, True Lavender

  L. latifolia (formerly L. spica) Spike Lavender or Spike,
  Portuguese Lavender

  L.×intermedia (formerly L. hybrida) Grosso Lavender, Lavandin

Patchouli (pach-oo-lee or puh-choo-lee) - amplifies the energy of
that around it, love, lust, sensuality, attraction, drawing

Pogostemon cablin (PO-goste-mon)

Thyme - loyalty, cleansing, attracts good opinions of others

Thymus vulgaris (TYE-mus)

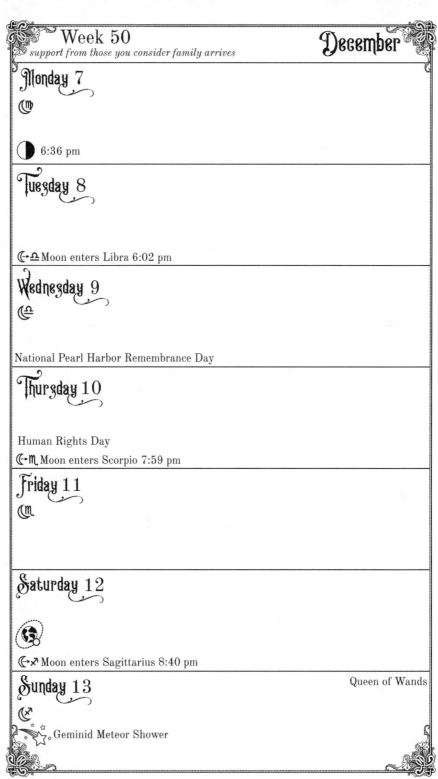

Monday 7
☾♍

◑ 6:36 pm

Tuesday 8

☾→♎ Moon enters Libra 6:02 pm

Wednesday 9
☾♎

National Pearl Harbor Remembrance Day

Thursday 10

Human Rights Day
☾→♏ Moon enters Scorpio 7:59 pm

Friday 11
☾♏

Saturday 12

☾→♐ Moon enters Sagittarius 8:40 pm

Sunday 13
☾♐

Queen of Wands

Geminid Meteor Shower

Rose - love, beauty, strength, protection, blessing

Rosa gallica var. officinalis (ROE-zuh GAL-ih-kuh var. uh-fiss-ih-NAY-lis) Apothecary's Rose

R. rugosa (roo-GOE-zuh) Hedge Rose, Hip Rose

Dill - money, protection, abundance, love, luck

Anethum graveolens (uh-NEE-thum)

Chives - protection, weight loss, healing

Allium schoenoprasum (AL-ee-um skee-no-PRAY-zum) Chives

Allium tuberosum (AL-ee-um) Garlic Chives

Oregano - extra energy and power, vitality, purification

- Origanum (uh-RIG-uh-num)
O. vulgare (vul-GAIR-ee) Oregano
O. vulgare subsp. hirtum (HUR-tum) Greek Oregano
O. dictamnus (dick-TAM-nus) Dittany of Crete
- Lippia graveolens (LIPP-ee-uh) Mexican Oregano
- Poliomintha bustamanta (poe-lee-oh-MIN-thuh bust-uh-MAN-tu) Mexican Oregano

Marjoram - dispells negativity, cleansing, dreams

Origanum majorana (may-jur-AY-nuh) Sweet Marjoram

Cinquefoil - love, money, health, power, wisdom, all-purpose herb to add energy to spells

Potentilla erecta (po -ten-TIL-uh) Five Finger Grass. Potentilla means powerful, referring to its numerous properties in wortcunning.

Chamomile - stress reduction, love, healing, calming, soothing
- Matricaria recutita (mat-ri-KAR-ee-uh) German Chamomile

Monday 14

● 10:16 am

☆ Geminid Meteor Shower

☾→♑ Moon enters Capricorn 9:35 pm

Tuesday 15

☾♑

Friday Gladheart's Birthday

Wednesday 16

☾♑

International Mountain Day
Conjunction of the Moon & Jupiter, view after sunset on the SW horizon

Thursday 17

☾→♒ Moon enters Aquarius 12:27 am

Friday 18

☾♒

Saturday 19

Ronald Hutton's Birthday
☾→♓ Moon enters Pisces 6:39 am

Sunday 20

☾♓

Queen of Cups
Queen of Pentacles

- Chamaemelum nobile (formerly Anthemis nobilis) English Chamomile, Ground Cover Chamomile

Clover - luck, money, lust, success, attraction

Trifolium pratense (try-FOE-lee-um) Red Clover

T. repens - White Clover

Lemon Balm - psychic development, love, money, success

Melissa officinalis (me-LISS-uh) Lemon Balm, Sweet Balm

-June

St. John's Wort - dreams & visions, banishing, protection, blessing, courage, vitality, optimism

Hypericum perforatum (hy-PEER-ih-kum)

Mullein - protection during dreams and astral projection

Verbascum blattaria (vur-BASS-kum) Moth Mullein

V. phoeniceum - Purple Mullein

Basil - love, money, exorcism, protection, sympathy

Ocimum basilicum (OH-sih-mum buh-SIL-ih-kum)

-July

Yarrow - divination, blessings, Handfastings, draws love

Achillea millefolium (ack-ih-LEE-uh mill-ih-FOE-lee-um)

Calendula - psychic powers, protection, legal matters

Calendula officinalis (kuh-LEN-dew-luh) Pot Marigold

Rowan - magical power, success, protection, strength, divination

Sorbus aucuparia (SORE-bus) European Mountain Ash, Rowan

-August

Verbena - protection, money, healing, sleep, purification, blessing

Verbena officinalis (vur-BEE-nuh) True Vervain, Herb-of-Grace

Monday 21

◑ 5:41 pm   4:02 am

☀→♑ Sun enters Capricorn 4:02 am
☽→♈ Moon enters Aries 4:33 pm

Tuesday 22
♈

 Ursid Meteor Shower

Wednesday 23
♈

Conjunction of Moon & Mars, view after sunset on the south-eastern horizon

Thursday 24

☽→♉ Moon enters Taurus 4:56 am

Friday 25
♉

U.S. Federal Holiday: Christmas

Saturday 26

☽→♊ Moon enters Gemini 5:33 pm

Sunday 27   King of Swords
♊   King of Wands

V. hastata - Blue Vervain, Simpler's Joy *(See page 16 to read about the Simpler's Method. This common name is from early American settlers. California's Concow Indians ate the seeds as pinole.)*

Mugwort - divination, purification, lust, fertility, sanity, dreams

Artemisia vulgaris[*] (compare to Sage from January) Mugwort

Mint - energy, vitality, alertness, success, money, communication
Mentha spicata (MEN-thuh spy-KAY-tuh) Spearmint
M. piperita - Peppermint
M. plegium - Pennyroyal
Monarda punctata (muh-NAR-duh punk-TAY-tuh) Horsemint
Nepeta×faassenii - Catmint

-September

Catnip - sleep, healing, dreams & visions, protection, love

Nepeta cataria (NEP-ih-tuh) Catnip *see Mint for Catmint*

Ginger - attracts opportunities and new adventures, love, lust

Zingiber officinale (ZING-gih-bur uh-fiss-ih-NAY-lee) Ginger

Asarum shuttleworthii (ASS-uh-rum) Wild Ginger

Asarum. virginicum (vur-JIN-ih-kum) Virginia Wild Ginger

Rue - protection, freedom, mental powers, anti-evil-eye

Ruta graveolens (ROO-tuh gruh-VEE-uh-lunz) Common Rue, Herb of Grace

Thalictrum aquilegiifolium (thuh-LICK-trum) Meadow Rue

-October

Comfrey - healing, luck, money, success, attraction

Symphytum×uplandicum (SIM-fit-um up-LAND-ih-kum)

---

[*]   The Artemisia species is named after the Goddess Artemis, and contains many amazing plants. In addition to the entries in January and August, there are many familiar herbs in this species such as tarragon, *A. dracunculus.* (druh-KUNK-you-lus). Artemisia are generally easy to grow and due to the silvery foliage of many herbs in the species, they make great additions to any Moon garden.

Monday 28
☽ ♊

Tuesday 29

○ 9:28 pm
☽→♋ Moon enters Cancer 4:29 am

Wednesday 30
☽ ♋

Thursday 31

☽☌♄ 3:56 pm
☽→♌ Moon enters Leo 12:58 pm

Friday 1
☽ ♌

U.S. Federal Holiday: New Year's Day

Saturday 2

☽→♍ Moon enters Virgo 7:13 pm
U.S. Federal Holiday: New Year's Day

Sunday 3
☽ ♍

King of Cups
King of Pentacles

Scullcap - sleep, dreams & visions, protection, binding oaths

    Scutellaria lateriflora (skoo-tuh-LAR-ee-ah) Scullcap

Jasmine - attraction, love, lust, "soul mates", wealth, divination

    Jasminum officinale (JAZZ-mih-num) Jasmine

    Jasminum nudiflorum (noo-dih-FLORE-um) Winter Jasmine

    Gelsemium sempervirens (jell-SEEM-ee-um sem-PUR-vur-enz) Carolina Jasmine

-November

Sandalwood - purification, protection, blessing, harmony

    Santalum album (SAN-tuh-lum AL-bum)

Cinnamon (SIN-uh-mom-um) -love, blessing

    Cinnamomum verum - Cinnamon

    C. aromaticm - Chinese Cinnamon

Cinnamon

Cayenne - cleansing, purification, banishing, adding power

    Capsicum species (KAP-sih-kum)

-December[*]

Frankincense - purification, blessing, consecration, meditation

    Boswellia carteri (boss-WELL-ee-uh) Frankincense

    B. seratta - Frankincense

Myrrh - healing, meditation, psychic abilities, attraction

    Commiphora molmol (kom-ih-FOR-uh) Myrrh

    Myrrhis (MIR-is) odorata Sweet Cicely, Myrrh

Bay - clarity, victory, business, purification, blessing, success

    Laurus nobilis (LORE-us NO-bil-iss) Bay Laurel bay laurel

---

[*]   If you find that you are drawn to the path of wortcunning, this list may be just a teaser. There are several plants of importance in magic and medicine that did not make this list. To delve further into this area, I suggest Mandrake (compare American and European), Anise (compare Anise Seed and Star Anise), Mistletoe, Veronica, Elder, and the extremely diverse and useful Viburnum genus.

Illumination of the Moon

The chart below makes it easy to understand the "three days" of the Esbats by showing you at a glance what percent of the face of the moon is illuminated at midnight. This visual appearance corresponds to the lunar energy. For most magical purposes any percentage above 97% can be regarded as **full**, and any percentage below 3% can be considered <u>new</u>.

Midnight* has been chosen as the time used in the chart below to take a quick snapshot of the percent of illumination. This is because most practitioners schedule their Esbats in the evening, although new Moon Esbats are sometimes held during the daytime when the Moon is overhead.

Date	Jan	Feb	Mar	Apr	May	Jun	Jul	Aug	Sep	Oct	Nov	Dec
01	32	42	35	48	54	74	81	94	99	99	100	99
02	41	52	44	59	65	83	89	98	100	100	98	97
03	51	62	54	69	76	91	95	100	99	98	94	92
04	60	71	65	79	85	97	99	100	96	95	89	86
05	69	80	74	88	93	100	100	97	92	90	82	78
06	78	88	83	95	98	100	99	93	86	84	73	69
07	86	94	91	99	100	97	95	88	78	76	64	59
08	92	98	97	100	99	93	90	81	70	68	54	48
09	97	100	99	98	95	86	83	73	61	58	43	36
10	100	99	99	93	90	78	75	64	52	48	32	26
11	100	94	96	86	82	69	66	54	42	37	22	16
12	97	88	91	77	73	60	57	45	32	27	13	08
13	92	79	82	68	63	50	48	35	22	18	06	<u>03</u>
14	85	69	73	57	53	41	38	26	14	10	<u>02</u>	<u>00</u>
15	75	58	62	47	44	32	29	18	07	04	<u>00</u>	<u>00</u>
16	65	47	52	37	34	23	21	10	<u>02</u>	<u>01</u>	<u>02</u>	<u>03</u>
17	53	36	41	28	26	16	13	05	<u>00</u>	<u>00</u>	06	09
18	42	26	31	20	18	09	07	<u>01</u>	<u>01</u>	<u>03</u>	13	16
19	31	18	23	13	11	04	<u>03</u>	<u>00</u>	05	09	21	24
20	22	11	15	07	06	<u>01</u>	<u>00</u>	<u>02</u>	11	17	31	33
21	14	05	09	<u>03</u>	<u>02</u>	<u>00</u>	<u>00</u>	07	20	26	41	43
22	07	<u>02</u>	04	<u>01</u>	<u>00</u>	<u>01</u>	<u>03</u>	14	30	36	51	53
23	<u>03</u>	<u>00</u>	<u>01</u>	<u>00</u>	<u>00</u>	04	08	23	41	47	60	62
24	<u>00</u>	<u>00</u>	<u>00</u>	<u>01</u>	<u>02</u>	10	16	33	52	57	70	71
25	<u>00</u>	<u>03</u>	<u>01</u>	04	06	18	25	44	63	67	78	79
26	<u>02</u>	06	<u>03</u>	09	12	27	36	56	72	76	85	86
27	05	12	07	16	20	38	47	66	81	84	91	92
28	10	18	13	24	30	49	58	76	88	90	96	97
29	17	26	20	33	40	61	69	85	94	95	99	99
30	25		29	43	51	71	79	91	97	98	100	100
31	33		38		63		87	96		100		99

* Midnight Central Time. For more information on calculating your local time zone if necessary, see the Time Zone Conversion pages.

Tarot

These interpretations were developed over decades of practice and thousands of readings. You can use these to supplement your own keywords for each card.

The first part of each meaning is for the upright position, but the essence of this meaning is always present no matter what position the card is drawn. The second part, marked with R:, is for the reversed or upside-down meaning of a card. Remember that the upright meaning still influences the reading, even when the card is reversed.

An example of this is the Wheel of Fortune drawn in reversed position. Most readers would say that this means "bad luck." However, luck can change, and just the mere presence of the Wheel indicates that things could be turned around. Look to the other cards in a spread (layout of tarot cards) to determine how this turn can occur.

- Major Arcana -

January

0 The Fool[*] Playfulness, Childlike, Adventurous, spontaneous **R:** Foolish - Naive - Overly Optimistic, not looking before you leap

I Magician Self Confidence, Arcana, secrets & occult study, Showmanship, show off, talented performer, meeting of fate **R:** Manipulation, Insecurity, Trickery, Lies, A Player

THE FOOL.

February

II High Priestess Experience, Wisdom, Intuition, psychic skills, Learning, Teacher **R:** Using knowledge without wisdom - Hysterical, unbalanced, out of control - Severe low self-esteem

III Empress Motherly, Growth, Nurturing, Abundance **R:** Shallow, Greedy - Ignoring the bigger picture - Motherly Problems

---

*   Technically, the Fool has no numeric designation and "travels" through the tarot. Many tarot scholars hold to the idea that the Fool must encounter every card in the deck to become enlightened. The Fool can be seen as both the first and the last card of the tarot but moves through cards too.

March

IV Emperor Order, rules, laws, authority figure, boss, getting organized **R:** Impractical, Narrow-minded, Control freak, need to get organized, a need to compromise

V Hierophant Following Tradition - Conventional - Getting good Counsel **R:** Counseling needed - Think for yourself - Unorthodox

April

VI Lovers Love & Romance, Sharing, Equal Partnership **R:** Separation, Arguments, Incompatible Partner

VII Chariot Travel, Movement, Drive, Ambition **R:** Procrastination, Delays, Obstacles, Can't move forward

May

VIII Strength Confident, In Control, Gaining Inner Strength **R:** Drained, Depression, Co-dependant, Fear of standing on your own

IX Hermit Meditation, Re-evaluate, Alone by choice Finding answers in yourself **R:** Unwanted loneliness, Need to re-evaluate, Isolation, Withdrawn, a need for introspection to gain insight

June

X Wheel of Fortune Prosperity, Promotions, Luck, Windfalls, Paid your dues **R:** Stuck in a rut, Refusing change, Not taking chances, Down on luck (but the wheel will turn again)

XI Justice Legal matters (good), Fair treatment, Karma **R:** Legal matters (disappointing or delayed), Unfair treatment

July

XII Hanged Man Suspension, Waiting, Calm before the Storm, Between **R:** Delays, Indecision. Hang Ups, Impatient

XIII Death Major changes - New outlook - Letting go **R:** Fear of change - Living in the past - Need to let go

August

XIV Temperance Patience, Compromise, Tolerance, Control, understanding degrees of intensity (a theft is not punished the same way that a murder would be) **R:** Need for moderation, patience or compromise, indulgence may be headed into addiction territory

XV Devil Obsession, Infatuation, Lust Materialism, Addiction **R:** Facing Fears - Overcoming all of the above

September

XVI Tower Chaos, Sudden Change (a needed change) Destruction **R:** Time to grow and move on, Rebuild with a clean slate

XVII Star Hope, Focusing on dreams & goals, Finding your true path **R:** Losing hope, Disillusioned, Depressed

October

XVIII Moon Something hidden from them or they are hiding something. Insecurity, Visions **R:** Deception, Something hidden (truth?) - Insecurity - Misunderstandings

XIX Sun New Beginnings, Success, Happiness, Birth, Children, Family **R:** Delayed beginnings, Feeling Unfulfilled, Family trouble

November

XX Judgement Good Karma, Rewards, Making fair and logical decisions **R:** Bad Karma, Poor Judgement, Be practical

XXI World Ending & New Beginning (School) Cycles, Success **R:** Delay in a Cycle Ending, need to accept changes, Complete projects before beginning something new

- Minor Arcana -

Swords: Conflicts, The Mind, Thoughts

Ace Beginnings, New Ideas, projects, Medical (surgery, injection, cut) **R:** Delays in new beginnings (cut out the past) Overbearing, Confusion, Medical(surgery, injection, cut), new ideas need more flushing out

Two Stubborn, No compromises, Battle of wills, Can't see a way out, Standstill **R:** Reconciliation, Compromise, Two things reuniting (ideas, people, etc.)

Three Love triangle, Jealousy, Heartache, Medical (surgery, injection, cut) **R:** Recovering from above, Medical (surgery, injection, cut)

Four Taking some "ME" time, Recovery, Rest, Take time off, Recuperate **R:** Recovery almost complete, Need to take some "ME" time

Five Finding out who your true friends are, Gossip, Deceit, Hidden or old enemies **R:** Finding out who your true friends are
Gossip ending, Truth revealed
Six Moving on, Letting go, travel, following your own path **R:** Frying pan into the fire - moving on in a bad direction
Seven Being Used, Theft, Trickery, lies, rip-off, doesn't trust (and maybe shouldn't) **R:** Not allowing yourself to be used, Evening the score, Stolen property returned
Eight Walking on eggshells, can't speak your mind **R:** Starting to speak your mind, Fear of independence
Nine Sleepless Nights, Worried, Stress, Illness? (reproductive system?) Worried Sick; Female Energy **R:** Light at the end of a tunnel, recovery, burden lifted, beginning to feel less stress
Ten Betrayal, Stab in the back, Landing flat on your face **R:** Learning from mistakes or betrayal, getting back on feet
Page Communicate, be direct to avoid serious misunderstandings, News (good) R: News (bad), Angry (with father?)
Knight Intelligent, changes coming quickly & unexpectedly **R:** violence, fights, sudden changes
Queen Sharp mind, sharp tongue, clever & helpful **R:** Bitter, mean spirited woman who knows just what to say to hurt you the most
King Sharp mind, sharp tongue, clever & helpful **R:** Nasty & mean spirited man, abusive

Cups, Goblets, or Chalices: Emotions, The Heart, Love & Relationships

Ace of Cups

Ace New relationships, birth **R:** New relationships delayed, next step delayed, pregnancy trouble
Two Equal and balanced relationship, feelings are mutual **R:** Unbalanced relationship, feelings are not reciprocated
Three Celebrations, parties, going out, no serious relationship, family gatherings **R:** Overindulgence, heavy partying, bad family gatherings, addiction

Four Not satisfied, not realizing the value of the current love, Bored **R:** Seeing the value of current love, becoming satisfied with a relationship, focusing too much on what has been lost rather than what exists

Five A loss but something left standing to rebuild on, focusing too much on the loss **R:** Same as above, but starting to focus on recovery

Six Family, memories, the past returning with new meaning **R:** Living in the past, outgrowing a relationship or person

Seven Too many dreams without plans to get them, choose a path or person, idealism **R:** Deciding what you want, making plans & setting realistic priorities, focusing on one path out of many options

Eight Leaving the past (loss & love) behind, some temporary loneliness **R:** Yo-yo relationships, settling for a relationship that isn't good

Nine Achieved goals and dreams, but now a bit bored **R:** Smug, Not quite accomplishing goals because they are unrealistic

Ten Wishes & Dreams coming true, love and family surrounding, comfort **R:** Happiness coming, but delayed, trouble getting a commitment

Page Loving person, student, Reflect & look inside yourself for inspiration & love **R:** Unloving person, need for reflection

Knight Love coming, Person who changes partners frequently **R:** Love going, past heartaches fading into the past

Queen Kind, gentle, soft-spoken, loving woman **R:** Hysterical, emotional, oversensitive, easily taken advantage of, unloving

King Fair, gentle, loving & caring man, great father figure **R:** Weak, unreliable man, cheater

TWO OF WANDS

Wands, Rods, or Staves: Communication, Ideas, Friendships, Expression of Thoughts, Movement

Ace New Creativity, Communication (letter, call, email) **R:** Feeling uncreative, uninspired, no communication (letter, call, email)

Two Best friendship, equal relationship, great communication, long-distance relationship **R:** Two people with different ideas and goals, incompatibility

Three Counseling, a third party helps (doctor, friend, shared work)

R: Third party interfering (inlaws, boss, etc.) Someone in the way

Four Stability, marriage, firm foundation **R:** Non-marital commitment, living together, living with roommates

Five Battles & arguments have good results, solutions found through fights **R:** Battles & arguments do not result in solutions

Six Victory, winning battles, overcoming stress **R:** Defeat, disillusioned, rewards and victory delayed

Seven Attacked from all sides, learning to communicate well & win battles **R:** Attacked from all sides and feeling drained & stressed

Eight Expanding horizons through travel, talking to people or seeing new places, reading new ideas **R:** Frustration and delays, can't seem to communicate, travel may be delayed or start late

Nine Battles are behind you now, ready & prepared for what is ahead, good at communicating **R:** Paranoid from many past battles, defensive (Jail? Prison?)

Ten Responsibilities you love to have, promotions, kids, rewards for hard work ahead **R:** Overburdened, too many responsibilities, rewards ahead - remain strong

Page Travel, news, communications, email, letters, phone calls **R:** Delays or problems in the above

Knight Person with an inner fire, great ideas, good at communicating **R:** Jumping from idea to idea, need for follow through

Queen Talkative & creative woman, full of fire and passion **R:** Gossipy, burns out quickly

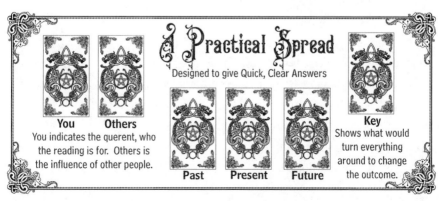

Practical Spread

Designed to give Quick, Clear Answers

You **Others**
You indicates the querent, who the reading is for. Others is the influence of other people.

Past **Present** **Future**

Key
Shows what would turn everything around to change the outcome.

King Talkative & creative man, very reliable and great to talk to **R:** Unreliable, forked tongue, smooth talker who is insincere

Pentacles, Coins, or Disks: Money, Material & Practical Matters

Ace New Job, Money coming, Ideas for making money, Begin new projects! **R:** Timing isn't right yet for new projects, Delays with money, news about money delayed or not as good as hoped

Two Juggling money or jobs, business partnership **R:** Trouble juggling money or jobs, distracted, borrowing from Peter to pay Paul.

Three Making money from an area of expertise, craftsmanship, journeyman **R:** Not using all your skills so not making the $ you could be

Four Financial stability, but too afraid to take risks or enjoy $ (insecurity) **R:** Greedy, stingy, extremely insecure and using money and material stuff as a security blanket

Five Feeling left out in the cold, worried about being broke, living paycheck to paycheck **R:** Recovering from emotional insecurity, temporarily unemployed, returning to work

Six Ask for what you need, loans, grants, gifts, inheritance (especially from family) **R:** Not getting help from others, having to pay back loans & debts, bad credit, no $ from family or bank

Seven Hard work leads to good $ and satisfaction **R:** Working hard but frustrated waiting for results, extra expenses coming up

Eight Learning a new skill & practicing will lead to a good financial state, apprenticing, creativity, education **R:** Losing interest in school or work, bored (refocus or learn a new skill before $ is lost)

Eight of Pentacles

Nine Making your home a retreat (not a fortress) remodeling, cleaning, buying a new home, gardening. $ is stable & growing **R:** Unexpected home repair or expense, blocking out the world, budget extra for living expenses, second mortgage being considered

Ten Money is good or will be soon. Secure and stable home & finances **R:** Major financial loss, may have to sell home or business, long term money is very good and secure because of this setback

Page News about $ (in the mail or by phone) young person beginning career **R:** Bad news about $, delays in beginning career

Knight Changing jobs, Person good with money and moving up in the world **R:** Unexpected change in job

Queen Practical, grounded, earthy & friendly **R:** Materialistic, gold digger, trouble handling practical money matters

King Good business sense, generous, grounded and practical **R:** Greedy, mean, unreliable, poor investment

---

* Picture adapted from the engraving entitled *A Dance of Shepherdesses* in the 1881 book M*usée Artistique et Littéraire*, Le, edited by J. Rouam.

Rune Directory

The Elder Futhark is often used for divination and personal reflection. Beside each rune below is its name followed by an approximate pronunciation and clues to its meaning in keywords and phrases. Use this as a quick reference or to start your study.

Fehu "fay-who": Controlled power over wealth. Manifesting creative energy and power. Invest wisely to increase wealth.

Uruz "ooo-rooze" Vital strength, primal power, determination health, perseverance, manifestation, wisdom & lore.

Thurisaz "thoor-ee-saws" Thorn, protection, fence, barrier, enemy of baneful forces, defense, destruction, applied power.

Ansuz "awn-sooze" Breath, word/song (as in words of power or incantations), shaping power or sound, expression, communication.

Raidho "rye-though" Riding, wheel, journey and travel, quest, change, ritual, rhythm, movement, order, underworld.

Kenaz "kane-awze" Torch, light, fires of transformation, passion, illumination, regeneration, enlightenment, kinship.

Gebo "gay-bow" Gift, exchange of powers, relationships, exchanges, crossing paths or uniting, connections, balance.

Wunjo "woon-yo" Joy, perfection, shared goals, harmony of like forces, the best traits of all involved combined as a force, happiness.

Hagalaz "haw-gaw-laws" Hail, hailstone, disruption, destruction, seed form, moving ice, enduring and overcoming hardships.

Naudhiz "now-these" Need, necessity, distress, necessity is the mother of invention, resistance, friction creates fire.

Isa "ee-saw" Ice, contraction, stillness, suspension, introspection, restraint, slowed growth (can be beneficial), stagnation.

Jera "yare-awe" Harvest, year, season, cycles, the flow of life-death-rebirth, fruition, completion, reaping what you sow.

Rune Directory

Runes can be used to inscribe tools, or to develop sigils for spellwork. It is best to develop a good understanding of the runes before such uses, and utilizing them as a divination tool will help you gain much insight.

Eihwaz "eye-wawz" Yew tree, axis of worlds, endings & beginnings, new opportunities, passages, between the worlds, protection.

Perthro "pear-throw" Dice cup, vulva, birth, problem solving, evolutionary force, "you buy your ticket-you take your ride".

Elhaz "ale-hawz" or "all-geese" Elk, protection, defense, support, luck, shielding, sanctuary, our connection with deity.

Sowilo "soe-wee-low" Sun, will, strength, victory, success, vitality, healing, solar energy and movement, directing power, clarity.

Tiwaz "tea-wawz" Creator, justice, success, responsibility, will, guided to success-truth-victory-justice-a good path, law & order.

Berkano "bear-kawn-oh" Birch tree, birch twig, life-death-rebirth, regeneration, growth, intuition, female fertility, new beginnings.

Ehwaz "ay-wawz" or "ay-woh" Horse, movement, connections, connecting with another force to move toward a goal.

Mannaz "mawn-nawz" Man (human), exams, disputes, challenges, arguments, gaining the upper hand, communication.

Laguz "law-gooze" Water, lake, flowing, emotions, intuition, psychic powers, revealing what is hidden (like beneath the water).

Ingwaz "eeeng-wawz" Fertility, Frey, potential energy, opportunity, how one thing ends affects how the next begins.

Dagaz "thaw-gauze" Day, a new day, new beginning, satisfactory or successful conclusion, positive end, final release.

Othala "oath-awe-law" Home, sacred ancestral land, inherited land, inheritance, ancestral power, true wealth and treasures.

Stones, Crystals & Minerals

Stones are excellent tools for spells and magic. You can use them in pouches, carry them as an amulet, incorporate them into tools, and use them as wards. This correspondence list will help you select the stone that fits your needs. These stone profiles reflect our experiences, so please remember that you may feel a different energy from a type of stone and that every stone has its own 'personality'.

Amazonite: A type of feldspar used for harmony, blending many energies, peace, calm, communication.

Amber: A powerful amulet and traditional Witch's 'stone' for good reason. The most ancient stone used for amulets and magic. Solar and light energy. Very energizing, increases power, purification, and protection from negativity, psychic and magical vampirism; shielding (without hiding).

Amethyst: Enhances general magical workings and raises personal power. To fine-tune its energy, combine amethyst with other stones and focus clearly on your goals and intent. Well suited to psychic development, protection, detoxification, inner exploration, emotional and psychic shielding, purification, breaking addictions, self-understanding.

Apache Tears: A special variety of volcanic obsidian used for protection and shielding, emotional cleansing, grounding. Brings protective earth energy to sensitive psychics and empaths.

Black Tourmaline: Protection and purification. Probably the best all-around protection stone. Tends to need less cleansing than many stones. Shielding, grounding, neutralizing, detoxification, prevents psychic and magical drain, anti-hex, converts negative energy into neutral energy.

Bloodstone: A red and green chalcedony used for strength, healing, courage, detoxification, purification. Very balancing, energizing and grounding of sexual and emotional centers for healing the body and spirit. Combines well with other stones and spell ingredients. (Works

Botswana Agate: Soothing and energizing, like a spa treatment for the spirit. For manifesting higher goals, clearing conflict, harmonizing, absorbs negative energy (cleanse stone well) and prevents unwanted visitors (physical, psychic, dimensional, etc.). Cuts ties to the past, psychic links, hexes, addictions & negative patterns. Helps prevent dwelling/obsessing on the negative; helps find solutions.

Carnelian: Orange-red and usually semi-translucent. For focus, concentration, uplifting, energizing, protection. Prevents psychic and emotional drain. Helps reinforce aura, increase confidence, improve motivation. Brings an energizing life force for creativity, personal will, and sexuality.

Celestite: Also known as Celestine, this rare mineral is used to help you connect with your higher self, tune-in to your deeper goals, face your shadows, and for dream work. Very healing when working through issues in order to reclaim your personal power, and open your flow of energy to that of the universe. With time, this use also helps with manifestation of your true goals and desires in the physical plane.

Citrine: A quartz in the yellow hues, from lemon-yellow to root beer amber. Very energizing and enlightening. Used for manifestation of creativity. Brightens mood, boosts your 'inner fire' and protects against negativity.

Clear Quartz: Power, protection, harmony, energy. These power-houses will boost the energy of any healing, energy work, ritual tool or talisman. Whether tumbled smooth or in their original pointed crystal form, they add their energy to the overall working according to your will and focus, while providing clarity and helping harmonize mixed energies of other stones, other people's wills, etc. Pictured is the crystalline growth of a cluster of crystals.

Fluorite: The color often indicates its uses, ranging from green (healing) to purple (psychic work) and more. Very high energy in the mind and crown chakra. It can help to open doors of perception, improve mental clarity for decision making, divination or study. Very cleansing and purifying, will remove negativity and is a great 'junk eraser' after healing, psychic, ritual, spell and magical work.

Garnet: Healing broken hearts, physical health, strength, sexual expression, self-worth, attraction, lust, sexual love, protection. Used to invoke the symbolism of the pomegranate. Earth energy, fertility.

Goldstone: Helps you focus on and achieve your goals; increases ambition and drive; emotionally stabilizing; protection; uplifting. Has a slight tendency to attract money.

Green Aventurine: A green quartz stone with mica inclusions. Increases opportunities, confidence, growth, personal energy, vitality, and perception. Aventurine is often used for luck; helping you take advantage of opportunities, and allowing you to better perceive opportunities as they arise. Traditionally used to attract adventure and for general attraction, creating a positive attitude, fortifying independence; said by some practitioners to invoke the favor of the Goddess of Love.

Hawk's Eye: A 'tiger's eye' stone in the colors of blue, green and gray. For clarity and gaining perspective, psychic work and visions, opening the third eye, protection while doing visualization, divination, and magic. Eye stones are often used for luck, helping you take advantage of opportunities, or helping you to perceive opportunities as they arise. Psychic, mental and emotional stamina.

Hematite: An iron oxide mineral. Manifestation, potency, charisma, grounding, balancing of opposites, detoxification, strength, and courage; can be used in spells for removing insecurity or even impotence.

Jasper: see Mook Jasper, Picture Jasper, Red Jasper

Jet: A very powerful amulet used since ancient times for protection, purification, manifestation on the physical plane, stress relief, dispelling negative patterns within and without, grounding (without heaviness). Prevents psychic and magical vampirism, purification, helps channel earth energies. Lunar and shadow energy. A traditional Witch's 'stone' with good reason.

Kyanite: Mental and psychic clarity; stays clear for better purification and protection; quick access to visualization, magickal powers, telepathy, and intuition. Unlocks the third eye, helps you understand how to use your skills responsibly. Aids in communication, expression, balance, dream work, meditation.

Lapis Lazuli: Creativity, visualization, expression, articulation, communication, intuition, useful for divination and psychic readings. Helps you tap into your psychic centers to aid in gathering and directing your energy, raising power for magick and spells, visualizing and manifesting goals.

Mahogany Obsidian: Promotes inner strength & healing; reduces feelings of unworthiness; amazing ability to end psychic attacks & psychic "chains" or "ties" placed either consciously or subconsciously by others. Stabilizing & grounding for better manifestation & healing. Unblocking, protection, gently grounding.

Malachite: Useful for analyzing repeated negative patterns, draws out repressed memories and emotions, good for revealing and healing emotional damage and trauma. Helps heal broken hearts.

Mook Jasper: A micro-crystalline quartz. Helps tune into earth energies, cycles, and patterns. Excellent for maintaining the sense of wonder and openness of youth, thereby increasing opportunities and a sense of gratitude.

Moonstone: Self-acceptance, self-confidence, tuning into your intuition and psychic centers, soothing, balancing and calming, dream work, shadow work, working with cycles and patterns, feminine power, intuition, Goddess energy, inspiration, creativity.

Picture Jasper: Banded with many colors, the patterns in the stone sometimes resemble a landscape. Tuning into earth energies, harmonizing multiple energies, gaining perspective and insight for physical manifestations (redecorating, garden plans, business plans). Visualization, nurturing, confidence.

Red Jasper: A micro-crystalline quartz. A very useful stone you will reach for again and again. Balancing, handling emotional stress, retaining dreams and visions, enhancing physical strength and inner stability. Gently grounding. Has good healing energy, especially in the lower chakra centers.

Red Tiger's Eye & Golden Cat's Eye: Found in red (tiger), gold and yellow (cat) and used for protection, perception, clear thinking, discovering the truth, and increasing luck. Like Aventurine, eye stones are often used for general luck, but this is primarily due to their ability to help you take advantage of opportunities by increasing your ability to perceive both opportunities and pitfalls as they arise. Excellent for enhancing and focusing your willpower, protection, grounding, vitality, motivation, balance, insight and integrity. Also used for psychic, mental and emotional stamina; and for seeing your way clearly.

Rhodonite: Pink and black coloration is a reminder of the grounding and centering of this stone's energy. It helps to stabilize emotions and ground the heart chakra for better healing. A stone of grace, discovering hidden talents, generosity, and compassion, expression of love, understanding your purpose.

Rose Quartz: Pink shades of micro-crystalline quartz, usually found in mass rather than individual crystals. Heals emotions, self-love & self-acceptance. Dissipates negativity, anger, tension & frustration. For unconditional love, self-acceptance, beauty, allowing love in, creativity; enhances receptivity to love; prevents fighting and encourages harmony, friendship, and peace. When combining multiple stones and crystals, rose quartz helps to harmonize their energies.

Ruby: Increases life force, courage, confidence; invokes sensuality and passion; attracts people towards the wearer. Energizes and activates all energy centers; Boosts motivation; helps aspire to new levels.

Sapphire: Balancing, healing & soothing; Increases awareness and personal power. Said to ensure faithfulness and protect relationships from love triangles

Selenite: A soft stone with a powerful punch. Helps to direct energy to your will and goals, aids in communicating with other realms, clears the cobwebs from the third eye and crown to enhance perception. Increase awareness, psychic skills & insight. Harmoniously blends & amplifies other stones.

Shiva Lingham: Meditation, insight, healing, very balancing & energizing, psychic skills, high spiritual vibrations, union of opposites, manifestation of wisdom. Healing of emotional and sexual issues, reclaiming sexual power and increasing self-love. Understanding and trusting the positive masculine.

Smokey Quartz: Protective of sensitive people, helping to guard against over-empathizing, being suckered by con artists, and helps prevent unhealthy relationships with others. Both grounding and uplifting, it is often used to move energy through all the seven major chakras. Pairs well with amethyst.

Shiva Lingam Stone

Snowflake Obsidian: Grounding, centering, protecting. Snowflake obsidian can help to bring hidden things to the surface. You can use this energy for emotional and physical healing, psychic awareness and even for spells to return lost objects. Helps one to see patterns for better psychic readings and mental health.

Sodalite: A fantastic writer's stone for inspiration and any creative pursuit involving intelligence, communication, education (teaching and learning), creativity, foresight, and logic.

Spirit Quartz: Found in amethyst, clear and other types of quartz, these special formations are a larger crystal covered in many smaller druzy quartz crystals. Gaining perspective, increasing humor and ability to experience joy, reducing fears and anxiety, moving on, speeds and enhances magical workings, great for covens as it helps many people work toward a common goal, heals discord, increases patience, will receive a magical charge well, making it well suited to talismans and wards. Projects a charge well.

Staurolite Crystal: Also called a *fairy cross*. Symbolizes the crossing of paths on the universal web, invokes the favor of the Fates or Goddess of Crossroads. Helps protect against hexes, negativity & rebound from magical work and spells.

Tiger Iron: A very powerful combination of red jasper, tiger eye, and hematite. Harmoniously blends all of the energies of these three stones. Great for manifestation, protection, energy, strength, stamina, increases willpower, motivation, bringing insights into action, healing, and grounding, creative solutions.

Tourmalated Quartz: A powerful shield of protection and neutralization of negative energy. Stays clear a long time, making it perfect as a 'take with you' charm. Energizing and grounding at the same time. Good for purification. The protective energy of tourmaline with the uplifting energy of clear quartz.

Tourmaline: see Black Tourmaline, Watermelon Tourmaline, and Tourmalated Quartz.

Unakite: A green and pink jasper (microcrystalline quartz) that balances and heals the heart, helps manifest love, calms, stabilizing, prevents ego-based negative patterns, releasing.

Watermelon Tourmaline: Balances the heart, encourages self-love while healing and recovering from negative relationships or past mistakes. Increases your magnetism and attraction for your positive benefit. Tends to protect you from spells cast by others, but this energy is more prominent in black tourmaline.

Wavellite: A powerful mineral found in Arkansas near the place where some of the best magical quartz crystals come from. Extremely useful for tuning into earth energies, manifestation, understanding interconnectedness, healing emotions, finding your path and making decisions. Excellent for healing, increasing your sense of well-being, changing your perspective when you are feeling down or 'stuck' and helps you gain insight.

Zebra Stone: Helps you see yourself and others clearly. Grounds high energy without being too heavy, it helps to manifest goals on the material plane. Unconditional love, helps harmonize varied energies of numerous stones or ingredients in a spell or talisman. Combats depression, apathy, and disinterest; increases creativity and motivation; nurturing & protective energy.

Color Magic

Color is incorporated into energy work in many different ways. A candle's color is chosen to help focus on the goal of spell working. If you are working on enhancing your psychic skills, you might choose a purple or violet cloth to wrap your tarot cards or a purple candle. You could also hold a purple amethyst or use a violet LED during meditation. Stone magic follows some of the associations of color magic, and learning Chakras is easier when you are familiar with the colors. E.g. Blue stones such as Lapis Lazuli, Sapphire and Celestite are used for psychic development and the third eye chakra. Each element is associated with a color, and these correspondences vary among Witches. The following are the most common associations. Extra space is provided for you to note your own intuitive associations alongside them.

Preparing a candle for magic by anointing it with oil is called "dressing" the candle. While dressing a candle, you focus your intentions while imbuing the candle with energy.

Color Associations

✪ **Red**: Lust, Passionate Love, Sexuality, Vigor, Magnetic, Virility

✪ **Pink**: Unconditional Love, Self Love, Beauty, Emotional (rather than physical) Love, Friendship

✪ **Orange**: Courage, Potency, Invigoration, Stimulation, Stamina

✪ **Yellow**: Intellectual Stimulation, Warmth, General Attraction

✪ **Green**: Fertility, Jealousy & Envy, Growth, Luck

✪ **Light Blue**: Healing, Soothing, Peace, Spirituality, Devotion

✪ **Dark Blue & Indigo**: Psychic Enhancement, Intuition, Wisdom

✪ **Violet**: Connection to the Divine, Spirituality, Air of Distinction, Expansion, Magic, Influencing Others

✪ **Black**: Absorbs, Banishing, Reversing Spells, Negativity, Grounding, Protection

✪ **White**: Protection, General Use, Peace, Purity, Tranquility

✪ **Brown**: Earth energy, Animals & Familiars, Grounding

✪ **Silver**: The Moon, Feminine Principle, Clairvoyance

✪ **Gold**: The Sun, Masculine Principle, Wealth

Glossary

Astrology: The metaphysical study of the influence of celestial bodies such as planetary positions or a person's zodiac sign.

Astronomy: The scientific study of space and celestial objects, and the physical universe.

Bane and Baneful: Bane is anything with an undesirable, contrary, or negative influence. Baneful magic is sometimes called "black magic."

Book of Shadows (BoS): A combination of journal, scrapbook, spells, rituals, recipes, and correspondences (such as your almanac's Directories). Many Witches keep a BoS, either printed or digitally, and they are very useful for keeping track of experiments and developing your personal path.

Cakes & Ale: Food and beverage used as part of a celebration. Usually, to show gratitude, ground out excess energy, or help practitioners bond during and/or after a ritual.

Deosil: Clockwise movement.

Divination: Using psychic abilities, intuition, and spiritual connection to determine (or "divine") insights into life's events, emotions, motivations, and the subconscious. Labeled "fortune-telling" by the layperson, divination is often practiced by the interpretation of signs and symbols. Various fields of techniques usually have ...*omancy* at the end of the word, i.g. cartomancy (divination by cards- tarot, playing, etc.), bibliomancy (divination with books), tasseomancy (reading tea leaves or other beverage sediments).

Dowser & Dowsing: Using a pointer, pendulum, or dowsing rod (branch or bent wires) to uncover what is obscured. I.g. - *A dowser came to our farm and witched (dowsed) for a spot for our new well. He used two copper dowsing rods that crossed over each other when he walked over the best spot to dig.* Visit the American Society of Dowsers at: https://dowsers.org

Initiation: Both a transitional phase (liminal) and a ritual. A candidate goes through a period of study and introspection before deciding to commit to a spiritual path. This period of time is traditionally a year and a day but varies among traditions. Solitary practitioners proceed at their own pace. A commemorative and transformative ritual is performed to acknowledge and embrace the initiate as a new practitioner, priest, priestess, etc. see also page 38 for initiation in regards to liminality.

Reversed Cards: A card is drawn in the upside-down position in a divinatory reading. Although the upright meaning is still present, it is modified by its inverted position. Keywords marked **R:** in your Tarot Directory indicate some of the meanings for these reversals.

Spread: Also called a **layout**. The pattern that cards are arranged to help specify what area is affected by each card. Example on page 133.

Widdershins: Counter-clockwise movement

Wortcunning: The art and science of working with herbs in brewing, cultivation, making medicines and other preparations, and knowing which herbs to use in what way for the best results (which may include magic).

Additional Notes

1 From the *Charge of the Goddess* by Doreen Valiente

2 Week numbers follow ISO-8601 standards and begin on Mondays, the Moon's day.

3 The Practical Witch's Almanac bypasses all confusion about New Moon vs. Dark Moon differentiations by using the scientific astrological data and the actual illumination of the Moon. No matter what path you walk, you can use the information in your Almanac to easily anticipate the actual energy of the Moon for any given date. For more, see the article *Dark Moons & New Moons*, the *Illumination of the Moon* chart, and your monthly *My Path* area.

4 Herbal study prompts use common names, but when you look under "Sage" in the Herb Directory, you will see that there are several "sages" listed. If you are not sure that wortcunning is your path, you can simply study the first herb on the list (in this example, Salvia officinalis). If you discover that you are enjoying your herbal studies, simply continue down the list of plants under each name. Whether you study one or all of the entries, by the time you finish the year's prompts, you will know some of the best and most versatile plants for magic, food, and medicine.

5 See the *2019 Practical Witches Almanac: Expanding Horizons* for more information about the Simpler's Menthod. ISBN: 9781621067313

6 Latin for "I shall find a way" from the longer Aut inveniam viam aut faciam or Aut viam inveniam aut faciam, "I shall either find a way or make one." A practical motto when Walking Your Path

7 As reported November 2018 in Newsweek, Pew Research Center conducted surveys that were released in 2014 showing that 0.4% of the U.S. population (1 to 1.5 million Americans) "identify as Wicca or Pagan." That means there are more Wicca or Pagan practitioners now than there are Presbyterians

8 There is a great little song that is sung or chanted around fires at Sabbats and festivals called *Who Were the Witches*. I found myself humming this song by Bonnie Lockheart as I compiled the hundreds of surveys we collected for this year's Almanac. It was obvious from these surveys that 90% of those who responded were solitary practitioners who do not attend group events. If this is the case for you, you might enjoy some of the songs often incorporated into these celebrations. Visit https://www.bonnielockhart.com/ to read the lyrics or listen to the sing-along version of the song off her 2002 "Dreams, Drums & Green Thumbs" album. One of my favorite versions of this song is by the Gaia Choir and can be found on YouTube at https://youtu.be/mb20WLM9Fds

9 When I was around six years old, my mother would tell me to stare at a blank white wall in order to find my own path. I didn't understand what I was supposed to do but continued this practice as a sort of meditation for many years. A kid has to do something during "time out", right? Later at University I had purchased a crystal sphere and was experimenting with scrying. I took a parapsychology class and found an obvious correlation to staring at a white field, scrying with a crystal ball, and the Ganzfeld effect we were studying in class. Later in the 90's I wrote about this in an article entitled *Scrying Without Crying* that has been republished online and offline. The idea has taken off since then, even being incorporated into the standard definition of scrying in books, articles, and encyclopedias. I don't believe that I was the first or am the only person to draw this correlation, and it may be one of Ken Keyes' Hundredth Monkey situations, but it is independent discoveries like this that help disciplines such as scrying develop and evolve. It is in this way that such disciplines are always modern and relevant.

10 The magical principles of this pendulum working are sound (using the hair and ring=contagion magic) even if the motivations are surprisingly outdated. In the 21st century, we are witnessing a welcomed end of such cisnormativity and the enforcing of gender roles onto our children. Even the concept of the family requiring a genetic connection has changed, and families are more often *chosen* now rather than genetically dictated. I last saw this done in 1989. See the Glossary, page 153 for Deosil/Widdershins.

11 A "Year and a Day" is a traditional term indicating the period of time a person dedicates to study and meditation prior to initiation into a degreed Witchcraft tradition.

12 *Officinalis* meaning "of the shop" is in reference to the species of a plant that was most historically used in apothecary shops for preparations and medicine.

Index

Answers to the Witchy Crossword

	Across		Down		Down
1.	perihelion	1.	mandrake	8.	cartomancy
2.	wormwood	2.	equinox	9.	aloe
3.	aura	3.	arcana	10.	arcana
4.	air	4.	broom	11.	eclipse
5.	libation	5.	earth	12.	apogee
6.	rede	6.	crone	13.	perigee
7.	umbra	7.	familiar	14.	esbat
8.	penumbra				

Downloads, Free Gifts & Calendar Apps

We are deeply grateful that you have choosen the Practical Witch's Almanac. In thanks for your patronage, many extras and bonus features are available to you on the PracticalWitch.com website.

- Printable Monthly Wall Calendars
- Access more Recipes, Spells, and Articles
- Download and Sync with iCal & Google Calendars
- Find last-minute dates for major Pagan festivals
- Printable Tarot Decks, Zener Cards, and Rune Cards
- Printable Book of Shadows pages & Psychic Worksheets
- Convert Almanac times to your local time zone
- Get Coupons, Horoscopes, Tarot Readings, and more

Just use page 82 to translate your login information below and visit

https://practicalwitch.com

Username: ⵣⵟⵓⵓⵟ   Password: ⵓⵟⵓⵟⵘⵏⵏⵣ

Credits & References

Your almanac was crafted using Open Source (OS) software, *Paint.net* and *Open Office*. OS is critical to the digital revolution so that creative expression and information sharing can be available to all. With OS, powerful tools that do not fall into obsolescence can be developed through collaboration, much in the spirit of true academia.

With the exception of the few credited images, all graphics, illustrations, and planner pages are made pixel-by-pixel. If they were drawn on canvas they would cover more than 235 square feet (about 22 m²). This labor of love is like painting with a brush 1/300th of an inch wide. Of course some elements such as the borders on the weekly planner pages only have to be drawn once and copied, but every effort is made to bring you a work of art that will bring daily charm and enchantment to your path.

All astronomical events are derived by referencing and cross-checking numerous sources for the greatest accuracy:

- U.S. Naval Observatory Database
- *Jet Propulsion Laboratory Development Ephemeris*: JPL DE430 from Pasadena, CA
- *The Swiss Ephemeris*: a highly precise ephemeris developed by Astrodienst, largely based on NASA's JPL DE431, released 9/2013.
- Moon Signs, Moon Phases, Sun Signs, etc. are cross-checked to longitude & latitude with *Daff Moon* Version 2.8 Copyright 2017 Evgeny Fedorischenk
- Meteor showers verification from: *American Meteor Society Ephemeris*
- Sunrise and set time verification from: the *ChronosXP* 4.1 program, version 4.1, developed by Robert Misiak
- Chinese New Year dates: *Chinese Fortune Calendar* and *Travel China Guide* online.
- Moon Signs: *The American Ephemeris* for the 20th/21st Century by Neil F. Michelsen
- Exact cross-quarter Sabbat dates are based on the more precise spacial method rather than splitting time intervals between Solstices and Equinoxes. They are interpolated as the midway points between the Solstices and Equinoxes measured in degrees along the ecliptic by former NASA scientist Rollin Gillespie as provided on the *Archaeo Astronomy* website-to which an annual donation is given in gratitude.
- Exact cross quarters are verified through various ephemeris and the writings of Arnold Barmettler and his work in computational astronomy.

Several individuals have helped in the creation of this almanac, and my gratitude goes to the team at PracticalWitch.com. Special thanks to Robert F. Jensen for his emotional and spiritual support, editorial input, and for providing me with enough coffee, chocolate, and time to complete this annual project while taking care of the practical matters at the PaganPath Sanctuary (home of the Practical Witch's Almanac). Thank you again, and may you have a magical and blessed year!   ~30~

Notes

Both standard and daylight times shown (s/d). Daylight Savings Time (DST) is already calculated for the U.S.A. For the UK and Western Europe, the times underlined between 29 March and 25 October should have one hour added to the GMT time to account for DST (Summer Time) in these areas. Example: 20 June Midsummer is 10:44 pm in London

Exact Sabbat Events	Hawaiian (HAs/dT)	Alaskan (AKs/dT)	Pacific (Ps/dT)	Mountain (Ms/dT)	Central (Cs/dT)	Eastern (Es/dT)	Atlantic (As/dT)	London (GMT)	Central Europe (CEs/dT)	Perth (AWT)	Sydney (AEs/dT)	New Zealand (NZs/dT)
Imbolc	Imbolc: February 3	February 3	Imbolc: February 4	February 4						February 4: Lammas		
	10:55 PM	11:55 PM	12:55 AM	01:55 AM	2:55 AM	3:55 AM	4:55 AM	8:55 AM	9:55 AM	4:55 PM	6:55 PM	9:55 PM
Ostara	Ostara: March 19						March 20	March 20		March 20: Mabon		
	5:50 PM	7:50 PM	8:50 PM	9:50 PM	10:50 PM	11:50 PM	12:50 AM	3:50 AM	4:50 AM	11:50 AM	1:50 PM	4:50 PM
Beltane	Beltane: May 4							May 5		May 5: Samhain		
	2:49 PM	4:49 PM	5:49 PM	6:49 PM	7:49 PM	8:49 PM	9:49 PM	12:49 AM	2:49 AM	8:49 AM	10:49 AM	12:49 PM
Midsummer	Midsummer: June 20	June 20								June 21: Yule		
	11:44 AM	1:44 PM	2:44 PM	3:44 PM	4:44 PM	5:44 PM	6:44 PM	9:44 PM	11:44 PM	5:44 AM	7:44 AM	9:44 AM
Lammas	Lammas: August 6	August 6						August 7	August 7	August 7: Imbolc		
	3:04 PM	5:04 PM	6:04 PM	7:04 PM	8:04 PM	9:04 PM	10:04 PM	1:04 AM	3:04 AM	9:04 AM	11:04 AM	1:04 PM
Mabon	Mabon: September 22	September 22								Sept. 22: Ostara		Sept. 23
	3:31 AM	5:31 AM	6:31 AM	7:31 AM	8:31 AM	9:31 AM	10:31 AM	1:31 PM	3:31 PM	12:31 PM	11:31 AM	1:31 AM
Samhain	Samhain: November 7	November 7								November 8: Beltane		
	12:56 PM	1:56 PM	2:56 PM	3:56 PM	4:56 PM	5:56 PM	6:56 PM	10:56 PM	11:56 PM	6:56 AM	8:56 AM	11:56 AM
Yule	Yule: December 21	December 21								December 21: Midsummer		
	12:02 AM	1:02 AM	2:02 AM	3:02 AM	4:02 AM	5:02 AM	6:02 AM	10:02 AM	11:02 AM	6:02 PM	8:02 PM	11:02 PM

Lunar Eclipses

When the Moon is entirely within the Earth's shadow it is a Total Lunar Eclipse. A Penumbral Eclipse happens when the Earth only obscures part of the Sun's light. Penumbral comes from the Latin *pœne* meaning *nearly* or *almost*, while *umbra* is Latin for *shadow*.

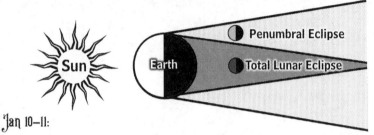

Jan 10–11:

Penumbral Eclipse, not visible in the United States.
Can be seen in the UK, Asia, Africa, Australia, and other areas.
Begins Jan. 10 at 11:08 am, Peak 1:10 pm, Ends 3:12 pm (CST).
In London it Begins at 5:07 pm, Peak 7:10pm, Ends 9:12 pm (GMT).

Jun 5–6:

Penumbral Eclipse, not visible in the United States.
Can be seen in the UK, Asia, Africa, Australia, and other areas.
In London it will be below the horizon until around suset. Begins
on June 5, 6:46pm, Peaks 8:25 pm, Ends 10:04 pm (BST)*.
CST: Begins June 5 at 12:47 pm, Peak 2:25 pm, Ends 4:05 pm.

Jul 4–5:

Penumbral Eclipse, is Visible in the United States, South America,
Most of Canada and Africa, and other areas. Begins July 4 at
10:08pm, Peaks 11:30 pm, Ends July 5 at 12:53 am (CST). In
London Begins July 5 at 4:07 am, Peak 5:30 am, Ends 6:52 am (BST)*.

Nov 29–30:

Penumbral Eclipse, is Visible in the U.S., Canada, Australia, South
America, Asia, and other areas. Begins 1:32 pm, Peaks 3:43 pm,
Ends 5:43pm (CST). In London it is only visible around sunrise.
Begins 7:32 am, Peaks 9:43 am, Ends 11:53 am (GMT).

Liber is Latin for book. You see why liber umbrarum might be a BoS.

London is on British Summer Time (BST) March 31 to Oct. 27, add 1 hour to BST for GMT

Solar Eclipses

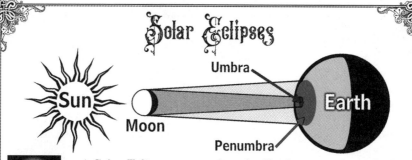

A Solar Eclipse occurs when the Earth passes through the shadow of the Moon. This can only occur during the New Moon when the Moon is overhead during the daytime. When the Moon's shadow (umbra) passes overhead while you are standing inside the umbra, you see a Total Solar Eclipse. When you are standing inside the penumbra, you see a Partial Solar Eclipse. However, in June of this year, the Moon is farther away in its elliptical orbit (near apogee) and only its penumbra will touch the Earth. This makes the Sun appear as a ring (annulus) and is called an Annular Solar Eclipse.

Unlike Lunar Eclipses that can be seen over a large hemisphere of the Earth, the path of the Solar Eclipse is a narrow band. From any one location, you will see about one Lunar Eclipse a year and a Total Lunar Eclipse about every three years. Total Solar Eclipses are much rarer, and you will only see one in any given location about every 360 years or more. Partial Solar Eclipses can be seen in most locations at least once every two years. The umbra of the Moon moves very quickly over the surface of the Earth causing a Total Solar Eclipse to last only about seven minutes, although the shade of the penumbra lingers much longer.

Total Solar Eclipses are an unlikely event. The Sun is 400 times larger than the Moon but it is also 400 times farther away from the Earth so its umbra is just the right size! Earth is the only place in our solar system with this symmetry, no other planet has Total Solar Eclipses. Jupiter's Partial Eclipses are caused by three Moons casting their shadows.

June 21: Annular Solar Eclipse, not visible in the United States.
Visible in Asia, Africa, parts of Australia and other areas.
Peak of Eclipse: 1:40 am CST, 6:40 am GMT, 7:40 am BST

December 14: Total Solar Eclipse, not visible in the United States.
Visible in South America, South-West Africa and other areas.
Peak of Eclipse: 10:13 am CST, 4:13 pm GMT

Notes

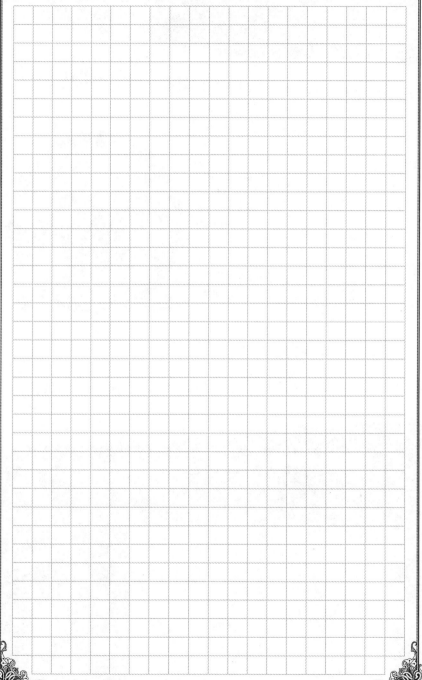

SUBSCRIBE TO EVERYTHING WE PUBLISH!

Do you love what Microcosm publishes?

Do you want us to publish more great stuff?

Would you like to receive each new title as it's published?

Subscribe as a BFF to our new titles and we'll mail them all to you as they are released!

$13-30/mo, pay what you can afford!

microcosmpublishing.com/bff

...AND HELP US GROW YOUR SMALL WORLD!

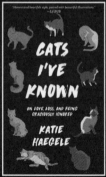